Crafting A Life: Readings to Feed the Soul

Cheryll L. Wallace

Copyright © 2012 Cheryll L. Wallace

All rights reserved.
Printed in the United States

Reprint Permissions appear
on page 352

ISBN 978-0-9852694-0-1

No part of this book may be reproduced without written permission from the author except parts of this book from The Retreats section that will be used in a specific retreat as outlined in this book.

Contact Cheryll Wallace at info@soulkitschn.com for permission to reproduce.

Need more copies? Contact us at
info@soulkitchn.com

To Benjamin --my son and my friend. Thank you for bringing such wondrous love into my life. You truly are my monument.
And
To Susan –my lover and my friend. Thank you for your supportive love. Not a day goes by that I do not marvel at your presence in my life.
And
To the members of First Unitarian Church in Omaha, Nebraska. Thank you for your love and encouragement from 1995-2011. You gave me a place to grow into the person I am today and for that I will be forever grateful.

There is danger that your mind may be frittered away by endless details, by listening continually to frivolous communications and suspicious complaints. To escape the narrowing influences, you should steadily devote a part of every day to solitary study; and, still more, you should make it your rule to regard the events and experiences of every day as lessons, and to strive to extract from them general truths, so that the intellect may enlarge itself in the midst of the humblest concerns.
-- William Ellery Channing

Table of Contents

Introduction	page 7
The Quotes:	
One	page 15
Two	page 28
Three	page 40
Four	page 53
Five	page 66
Six	page 78
Seven	page 88
Eight	page 102
Nine	page 112
Ten	page 125
Eleven	page 140
Twelve	page 151
The Retreats:	page 162
Retreat One	
Openness	page 163
Closing Ritual Activities:	175
Closing Readings:	178
Retreat Two	
Hospitality	page 186
Retreat Three	
Connection	page 200

Retreat Four Imagination	page 212
Retreat Five Gratitude	page 227
Retreat Six Silence	page 239
Retreat Seven Wonder	page 254
Retreat Eight Play	page 266
Retreat Nine Shadow	page 278
Retreat Ten Mindfulness	page 288
Retreat Eleven Listening	page 302
Retreat Twelve Justice	page 316
Author Index	page 326
Subject Index	page 340
Permissions	page 352

Introduction

I was not taught how to choose the life I wanted when I was growing up. I thought you took what you got. I pretty much did just that until my early 30s when one day I woke up and realized that there was a big exciting world out there and my life could be more than what I had settled for so far. It was the beginning of a rewarding adventure that is still unfolding. Through the years as I have explored various spiritual paths, words of wisdom - hallowed through the ages - have become my guides, my energizers, my friends. Through the use of quotes and short readings I have learned how to listen to my soul trying to sing its unique song through the use of my physical body.

THE WRITINGS
"Holy Reading" as a spiritual practice

From ancient times until the present, holy reading has been practiced as a contemplative way to read scripture but holy reading does not have to be used only with traditional scripture. This type of reading is about letting a passage speak to you in a way that goes beyond head knowledge to a knowing that is soul deep. St. Benedict encouraged this habit as a way to "hear with the heart." The first step in sacred reading is silence. If we are surrounded by noise or constantly speaking, we will be unable to hear the passage speak to us. The next step is to read a passage and then ruminate on it. Ruminants are animals that chew their cud. They partially chew the food and send it to one stomach, retrieving it later to chew it in its entirety and send it to the digestive stomach. Another way to express this concept would be to reflect on the passage. The next step is to experience the reading. This can be done by allowing the passage to speak to our deepest dreams and fears and by applying the reading to current or past situations in our lives….by living with the passage for a few days and rolling it over in our minds and hearts, peeling off the meanings layer by layer. The final step is to allow the ways in which the passage spoke to you to take root in your life and grow there. In this way the passage becomes a sacred part of your life— a treasure to enrich, inspire and console.

THE PRACTICE

As with any new learning, there are things you can do to make sure that you are available to hear what the passage or image you have chosen is speaking to you:

- treat your sacred reading/reflection time as you would time with a dear friend
- prepare a quiet, comfortable space, with as few distractions as possible- turn off phones and close the door
- take time with your reading or drawing and be patient as you allow its message to speak to you
- if this copy of *Crafting A Life* is yours, make notes in the margins and underline important words for future reflection
- have a conversation in your mind or on paper with the author of the reading, or the Divine, or yourself, as to the meaning of the reading or drawing
- journal or draw, or insert yourself into the reading as one of the characters, to further explore the passages you have chosen

- discuss the readings and drawings with others and share your insights, making sure to listen to theirs as well

THE DRAWINGS

In addition to quotes and stories, I have included some of my original ink drawings in this book for your contemplation. Most of the drawings do not contain recognizable objects and are nothing more than a series of shapes fit together to create a whole design. There is no one right way to interpret them. They are meant as objects of reflection. Look at the drawing as a whole and also at the individual pieces and let it speak to you. I cannot tell you more than that, really. You may pick out shapes that look like recognizable objects to you, even when they weren't meant to resemble those things. That's fine. The important thing is to look at the drawing, at most, for what it might reveal to you, and at least, as a pleasing image where your imagination can romp.

THE RETREATS

In the back of the book you will find 12 retreat ideas, one for each month. They don't have to be done in any order and Retreat One does not have to correspond to January, etc. I would encourage you to take one day, or at least one portion of a day each month, to spend in time alone or with a small group of spiritual friends for a lengthier reflection. Think of it as re-creation. All of the retreats follow a basic outline that can be fleshed out to whatever extent you have the time to spend. Readings and ideas for further exploration are included in each retreat plan. It is my hope that these intentional soul vacations will help you to enrich your journey, both in the relationship with yourself and with the friends who walk the path with you.

However you choose to use this book, slow down and take your time with the treasures contained in its pages. Listening as the selections speak to you will open your mind to possibilities you might not otherwise have seen. In spiritual practice, the purpose is not perfection but practice...keeping at it...staying engaged in life by paying attention. As you slow down, may you find the time to feed your soul and to live the life you long to live instead of the life you have fallen into the habit of living.

I believe that life is about the journey much more than the destination. Every little awareness we have and every little step we take helps us to know more about ourselves and our connectedness to others. So enjoy... and may this book help you to open yourself to the gifts of the journey as you craft the gift that is your life.

Peace Be With You,

Cheryll Wallace
March 2012

THE WRITINGS and THE DRAWINGS

ONE

1. We are stuck between the past and the future. The past is no longer in our hands. Neither is the future since it doesn't exist yet. The only time we have control over is the present. It is now, it exists. It's not heavy to bear, and it's livable by all, on one condition: that we let the past go, and not be impatient for the future. The present moment passes quickly; before you know it, it's in the past while another present takes its place, as light and narrow and fleeting as the preceding one.
— Michael Quoist

2. A great Sufi teacher told of the time when Jesus went for a walk and was insulted by some townsfolk. Jesus responded by including these people in his prayers. "Why didn't you answer their insults?" a disciple asked. Jesus replied, "I can only pay people back with coins I have in my purse."
— Author Unknown

3. When the shoe fits, the foot is forgotten.
When the belt fits, the belly is forgotten.
When the heart is right, "for" and "against" are forgotten.
— Chuang Tzu

4. It was a dangerous thing to do, for those who enter the heart of a sacred question and feel the searing heat it gives off are usually compelled to live on into the answer.
— Sue Monk Kidd

5. It was a chilly, overcast day when the horseman spied the little sparrow lying on its back in the middle of the road. Reining in his mount he looked down and inquired of the fragile creature,
"Why are you lying upside down like that?"
"I heard the heavens are going to fall today," replied the bird.
The horseman laughed. " And I suppose your spindly legs can hold up the heavens?"
"One does what one can," said the little sparrow.
— Author Unknown

6. When we speak directly to others in order to achieve a goal, we feel the anxiety that comes from trying to exercise influence. But when we speak, free of the need to achieve a result, we feel energized and at peace.
— Parker Palmer

7. To have courage for whatever comes in life, everything lies in that.
— Teresa of Avila

8. When Akiba was on his deathbed, he bemoaned to his rabbi that he felt he was a failure. His rabbi moved closer and asked why, and Akiba confessed that he had not lived a life like Moses. The poor man began to cry, admitting that he feared God's judgment. At this, his rabbi leaned into his ear and whispered gently, "God will not judge Akiba for not being Moses. God will judge Akiba for not being Akiba."
— From *The Talmud*

9. If you want to be truly understood, you need to say everything three times, in three different ways. Once for each ear…and once for the heart.
— Paula Underwood Spencer

10. We have become not a melting pot but a beautiful mosaic.
Different people, different beliefs, different yearnings,
different hopes, different dreams.
— Jimmy Carter

11. Wanting to reform the world without discovering one's true self is like trying to cover the world with leather to avoid the pain of walking on stones and thorns.
It is much simpler to wear shoes.
— Ramana Maharshi

12. I understand hell in two ways. First, there is the this-worldly hell I make for myself and others when I fail to act justly and with compassion. Second, there is the other-worldly hell invented by bullies who delight in sadistic fantasies of endless torture and use these fantasies to frighten others into yielding to their will. I take both hells very seriously.
— Rabbi Rami Shapiro

13. And then the day came when the risk to remain tight in a bud was more painful than the risk to bloom.
— Anaïs Nin

14. Wisdom tells me I am nothing.
Love tells me I am everything.
And between the two my life flows.
— Nisargadatta Maharaj

15. Do all your duties but keep your mind on God.
Live with all and serve them. Treat them as if they were very dear to you, but know in your heart of hearts that they do not belong to you… The tortoise moves about in the water. But can you guess where her thoughts are? They are on the bank where her eggs are lying. Do all your duties in the world but keep your mind on God.
— Ramakrishna

16. So many of our dreams at first seem impossible,
then they seem improbable,
and then, when we summon the will, they soon become inevitable.
— Christopher Reeve

17. Lord, make me an instrument of your peace:
Where there is hatred, let me sow love;
Where there is injury, pardon;
Where there is doubt, faith;
Where there is despair, hope;
Where there is darkness, light;
Where there is sadness, joy.
O Divine Master, grant that I may not so much seek to be consoled
as to console;
To be understood, as to understand;
To be loved, as to love.
For it is in giving that we receive,
It is in pardoning that we are pardoned,
It is in dying to self that we are born again.
— Francis of Assisi

18. The higher goal of spiritual living is not to amass a wealth of information, but to face sacred moments.
— Abraham Heschel

19. The first peace, which is the most important, is that which comes within the souls of men when they realize their relationships, their oneness, with the universe and all its powers, and when they realize that at the center of the universe dwells Wakan-Tanka, the Supreme Being, and that this center is really everywhere, it is within each of us…there can never be peace between nations until there is... first... that true peace within the souls of men.
— Black Elk

20. The more faithfully you listen to the voice within you, the better you will hear what is sounding outside. And only he who listens can speak. Is this the starting point of the road towards the union of your two dreams— to be allowed in clarity of mind to mirror life and in purity of heart to mold it?
— Dag Hammarskjold

21. The most important word in our language is yes.
It matters what we say yes to.
It matters what we say no to.
Every no gets its value from the yes it also affirms.
To say no to what denies and destroys is also to say yes to what affirms, builds, creates.
— Jacob Trapp

22. Let us plant dates even though those who plant them will never eat them.
We must live by the love of what we will never see. This is the secret discipline. It is a refusal to let the creative act be dissolved away in immediate sense experience, and a stubborn commitment to the future of our grandchildren. Such disciplined love is what has given prophets, revolutionaries, and saints the courage to die for the future they envisaged. They make their own bodies the seed of their highest hope.
— Ruben Alves

23.   Do not be too moral. You may cheat yourself out of much life. Aim above morality.
Be not simply good; be good for something.
— Henry David Thoreau

24.   Finish each day and be done with it. You have done what you could; some blunders and absurdities have crept in; forget them as soon as you can.
Tomorrow is a new day; you shall begin it serenely and with too high a spirit to be encumbered with your old nonsense.
— Ralph Waldo Emerson

25.   There is a voice inside of you
That whispers all day long,
"I feel that this is right for me,
I know that this is wrong."
No teacher, preacher, parents, friend,
or wise man can decide
what's right for you —
Just listen to
the voice that speaks inside.
— Shel Silverstein

26. The real voyage of discovery consists not in seeking new landscapes but in having new eyes.
— Marcel Proust

27. A wise woman who was traveling in the mountains found a precious stone in a stream. The next day she met another traveler who was hungry, and the wise woman opened her bag to share her food. The hungry traveler saw the precious stone and asked the woman to give it to him. She did so without hesitation.
The traveler left, rejoicing in his good fortune. He knew the stone was worth enough to give him security for a lifetime. But a few days later he came back to return the stone to the wise woman.
"I've been thinking," he said, "I know how valuable the stone is, but I give it back in the hope that you can give me something even more precious. Give me what you have within you that enabled you to give me the stone."
— Author Unknown

28. I've learned that you can tell a lot about a person by the
way she handles these three things:
a rainy day, lost luggage, & tangled Christmas tree lights.
— Maya Angelou

29. I think the real miracle is not to walk either on water or in thin air,
but to walk on earth.
— Thich Nhat Hanh

30. The most beautiful thing we can experience is the mysterious.
It is the source of all true art and all science. He to whom this emotion is a stranger,
who can no longer pause to wonder and stand rapt in awe, is as good as dead: his eyes are closed.
— Albert Einstein

31. They say that time changes things, but you actually have to change them yourself.
— Andy Warhol

TWO

1.   It is one of the most beautiful compensations of life that no woman or man can sincerely try to help another without helping her or himself.
— Ralph Waldo Emerson

2.   But suppose God is black? What if we go to Heaven and we, all our lives, have treated the Negro as an inferior, and God is there, and we look up and He is not white?
What then is our response?
— Robert F. Kennedy

3.   There is no not-holy. There is only that which has not yet been hallowed, which has not yet been redeemed to its holiness.
— Martin Buber

4. A rock pile
ceases to be
a rock pile the moment
a single man
contemplates it,
bearing within him the
image of a cathedral.
— Antoine De Saint-Exupery

5. At each moment you choose the intentions that will shape your experiences
and those things upon which you will focus your attention.
— Gary Zukov

6. You will find, as you look back upon your life, that the moments when you have truly lived are the moments when you have done things in the spirit of love.
— Henry Drummond

7.   We look at some people as if they were special, gifted, divine.
Nobody is special and gifted and divine.
No more than you are, no more than I am.
The only difference, the very only one,
is that they have begun to understand what they really are
and have begun to practice it.
— Richard Bach

8.   Cherish no hate for thy brother who offends,
because you have not offended like him.
If your fellow man possessed your nature,
he might not have sinned.
If you possessed his nature,
you might have offended as he has done.
A man's transgressions depend not entirely upon his free choice,
but often upon many other circumstances.
— from the Hindu tradition

9. I've learned that you shouldn't go through life with a catcher's mitt on both hands;
you need to be able to throw some things back.
— Maya Angelou

10. There is no immunity from being touched by the vast diversity
of every possible sin.
(If sin exists, everybody has a little of it.)
— Susan Murphy

11. The truth is that there is nothing noble in being superior to somebody else. The only real nobility is in being superior to your former self.
— Whitney Young

12. The important thing is this:
To be able at any moment to sacrifice what we are
for what we could become.
— Charles Dubois

13. One evening an old Cherokee told his grandson about a battle that goes on inside people. He said, "My son, the battle is between two "wolves" inside us all.

One is Evil. It is anger, envy, jealousy, sorrow, regret, greed, arrogance, self-pity, guilt, resentment, inferiority, lies, false pride, superiority, and ego.
The other is Good. It is joy, peace, love, hope, serenity, humility, kindness, benevolence, empathy, generosity, truth, compassion and faith."

The grandson thought about it for a minute and then asked his grandfather: "Which wolf wins?" The old Cherokee simply replied, "The one you feed."
— from the Cherokee tradition

14. Only those who will risk going too far can possibly find out how far one can go.
— T. S. Eliot

15. The true measure of a person is how one treats someone
who can do them absolutely no good.
 — Ann Landers

16. The main thing
is to keep the main thing
the main thing.
 — Stephen Covey

17. Whether a person makes a living casting stones into the sea
or as a priest in the temple makes no difference to God.
 — Ramakrishna

18. Why not let people differ about their answers to the great mysteries of the Universe? Let each seek one's own way to the highest, to one's own sense of supreme loyalty in life, one's ideal of life. Let each philosophy, each worldview bring forth its truth and beauty to a larger perspective, that people may grow in vision, stature, and dedication.
 — Algernon Black

19. If you cannot be a poet,
be the poem.
— David Carradine

20. A hundred times a day I remind myself
that my inner and outer life depend on
the labors of other men, living and dead,
and that I must exert myself in order to
give in the measure as I have received
and am still receiving.
— Albert Einstein

21. Love the animals, love the plants,
love everything. If you love everything,
you will perceive the divine mystery in
things. Once you perceive it, you will
begin to comprehend it better every day.
And you will come at last to love the
whole world with an all-embracing love.
— Fyodor Dostoyevsky

22. For a long time it had seemed to me that life was about to begin— real life.
But there was always some obstacle in the way, something to be gotten through first, some unfinished business, time still to be served, a debt to be paid.
Then life would begin.
At last it dawned on me that these obstacles were my life.
— -Alfred D. Souza

23. Past the seeker as he prayed came the crippled and the beggar and the beaten. And seeing them...he cried, "Great God, how is it that a loving creator can see such things and yet do nothing about them?"
God said, "I did do something. I made you."
— From the Sufi tradition

24. If you hear a voice within you say "you cannot paint,"
then by all means paint, and that voice will be silenced.
— Vincent Van Gogh

25. Faith is sometimes the irrational season
Where love for God blooms bright and wild.
Had Mary been filled with reason,
There may not have been room for the child.
— Madeleine L'Engle

26. The truth is that our finest moments are most likely to occur
when we are feeling deeply uncomfortable, unhappy, or unfulfilled.
For it is only in such moments, propelled by our discomfort,
that we are likely to step out of our ruts and start searching for different ways
or truer answers.
— M. Scott Peck

27. When a man finds no peace within himself,
it is useless to seek it elsewhere.
— L. A. Rouchefolicauld

28. There are spaces between our fingers
So that another person's fingers can fill them in.
— a Hindu Proverb

29. I think most of the spiritual life is really a matter of relaxing —
letting go, ceasing to cling, ceasing to insist on our own way,
ceasing to tense ourselves up for this or against that.
— Beatrice Bruteau

30. Use what talent you possess:
the woods would be very silent
if no birds sang except those that sang best.
— Henry Van Dyke

31. We often think of peace as the absence of war; that if the powerful countries would reduce their arsenals, we could have peace. But if we look deeply into the weapons, we see our own minds — our prejudices, fears, and ignorance. Even if we transported all the bombs to the moon, the roots of war and the reasons for bombs would still be here, in our hearts and minds, and sooner or later we would make new bombs. Seek to become more aware of what causes anger and separation, and what overcomes them. Root out the violence in your life, and learn to live compassionately and mindfully.
— Thich Nhat Hanh

THREE

1.   There are only two ways to live your life.
One is as though nothing is a miracle.
The other is as though everything is a miracle.
— Albert Einstein

2.   Strive constantly to serve the welfare of the world;
by devotion to selfless work one attains the supreme goal of life.
Do your work with the welfare of others always in mind.
— *The Bhagavad Gita* 3:19-20

3.   You can discover more about a person in an hour of play
than in a year of conversation.
— Plato

4.   In any moment of decision the best thing you can do is the right thing,
the next best thing is the wrong thing,
and the worst thing you can do is nothing.
— Theodore Roosevelt

5. Kindness is in our power, even when fondness is not.
— Samuel Johnson

6. True peace is not merely the absence of tension,
it is the presence of justice.
— Martin Luther King, Jr.

7. Our Father, Mother, who are in the world and surpass the world,
Blessed be your presence, in us, in animals and flowers, in still air and wind.
May justice and peace dwell among us, as you come to us.
Your will be our will.
You will that we be sisters and brothers, as bread is bread, water is itself,
for our hunger, for quenching of thirst.
Forgive us.
We walk crookedly in the world, are perverse, and fail of our promise.
But we would be human, if only you consent to stir up our hearts.
Amen
— Daniel Berrigan

8. Nearly all men can stand adversity, but if you want to test a man's character, give him power.
— Abraham Lincoln

9. Never let your sense of morals prevent you from doing what's right.
— Isaac Asimov

10. We need spiritual heroes to give us working images of different types of sanctified lives that we can hold before our eyes for inspiration.
— Sam Keen

11. I offer you love.
I offer you friendship.
I see your beauty.
I hear your need.
I feel your feelings.
My wisdom flows from the Highest Source.
I salute that Source in you.
Let us work together for unity and love.
— Mahatma Gandhi

12.   Millions long for immortality who do not know what to do with
themselves on a rainy Sunday afternoon.
— Susan Ertz

13.   I had always wanted an adventurous life. It took a long time to realize that I was the only one who was going to make an adventurous life happen to me.
— Richard Bach

14.   Our lives are filled with ordinary moments when
the hidden beauty of life breaks into our everyday awareness
like an unbidden shaft of light.
It is a brush with the sacred, a near occasion of grace.
Too often we are blind to these moments.
We are busy with our daily obligations and too occupied
with our comings and goings to surround our hearts
with the quiet that is necessary to hear life's softer songs.
— Kent Nerburn

15.   We cannot live only for ourselves.
A thousand fibers connect us….
and among those fibers, as sympathetic threads,
our actions run as causes and they come back to us as effects.
On a daily basis, we affect the web of all existence, just as we are affected by it.
— Herman Melville

16.   The beginning of love is to let those we love be perfectly
themselves, and not to twist them to fit our own image.
Otherwise we love only the reflection of ourselves we find of them.
— Thomas Merton

17.   Call it a clan, call it a network, call it a tribe, call it a family.
Whatever you call it, whoever you are, you need one.
— Jane Howard

18.   A stranger is shot in the street, you hardly move to help. But if, half an hour before, you spent just ten minutes with the fellow and knew a little about him and his family, you might just jump in front of his killer and try to stop it.
Really, knowing is good.
Not knowing, or refusing to know is bad, or amoral, at least.
You can't act if you don't know.
— Ray Bradbury

19.   Being a saint is simply being the person God made me to be. Saints, at the end of the day, are not really strange or odd or misfits. They are simply real, or normal. They actually are what we are all made to be, what we can be.
— James C. Howell

20. When I was young and free and my imagination had no limits, I dreamed of changing the world. As I grew older and wiser, I discovered the world would not change, so I shortened my sights somewhat and decided to change only my country. But it too seemed immovable. As I grew into my twilight years, in one last desperate attempt, I settled for changing only my family, those closest to me, but alas they would have none of it. And now, as I lie on my deathbed, I suddenly realize: If I had only changed myself first, then by example I would have changed my family. From their inspiration and encouragement, I would then have been able to better my country and who knows, I may have even changed the world.
— on the tomb of an Anglican Bishop in Westminster Abbey

21. Hear me, four quarters of the world — a relative I am!
Give me the strength to walk the soft earth, a relative to all that is!
Give me the eyes to see and the strength to understand, that I may be like you.
With your power only can I face the winds.
— Black Elk

22. Thousands of years ago the question was asked; "Am I my brother's keeper?" That question has never yet been answered in a way that is satisfactory to civilized society. Yes, I am my brother's keeper. I am under a moral obligation to him that is inspired, not by any maudlin sentimentality but by the higher duty I owe myself. What would you think of me if I were capable of seating myself at a table and gorging myself with food and saw about me the children of my fellow beings starving to death?
— Eugene V. Debs

23. How can God direct our steps if we're not taking any?
— Sarah Leah Grafstein

24. The human soul has need of security and also of risk. The fear of violence or of hunger or of any other extreme evil is a sickness of the soul. The boredom produced by a complete absence of risk is also a sickness of the soul.
— Simone Weil

25. Being a saint is simply being the person God made me to be. Saints, at the end of the day, are not really strange or odd or misfits. They are simply real, or normal. They actually are what we are all made to be, what we can be.
— James C. Howell

26.   If you were all alone in the universe with no one to talk to, no one with which to share the beauty of the stars, to laugh with, to touch, what would be your purpose in life?
It is other life, it is love, which gives your life meaning.
This is harmony.
We must discover the joy of each other, the joy of challenge, the joy of growth.
— Mitsugi Saotome

27.   The opposite of love is not hate, it's indifference.
The opposite of art is not ugliness, it's indifference.
The opposite of faith is not heresy, it's indifference.
And the opposite of life is not death, it's indifference.
— Elie Wiesel

28.   Tell me, what is it you plan to do with your one wild and precious life?
— Mary Oliver

29. Many people die with their music still in them.
Why is this so?
Too often it is because they are always getting ready to live.
Before they know it, time runs out.
— Oliver Wendell Holme

30. He alone sees truly who sees the Lord the same in every creature… seeing the same Lord everywhere, he does not harm himself or others.
— Lord Krishna in *The Bhagavad Gita*

31. A human being is a part of the whole called by us universe,
a part limited in time and space.
He experiences himself, his thoughts and feelings
as something separated from the rest, a kind of optical delusion of his consciousness.
This delusion is a kind of prison for us, restricting us to our personal desires
and to affection for a few persons nearest to us.
Our task must be to free ourselves from this prison
by widening our circle of compassion to embrace all living creatures and the whole of nature in its beauty.
— Albert Einstein

FOUR

1. Whatever affects one directly, affects all indirectly.
I can never be what I ought to be until you are what you ought to be.
This is the interrelated structure of reality.
— Martin Luther King, Jr.

2. As is the human body, so is the cosmic body.
As is the human mind, so is the cosmic mind.
As is the microcosm, so is the macrocosm.
As is the atom, so is the universe.
— From *The Upanishads*

3. At the deepest level of ecological awareness
you are talking about spiritual awareness.
Spiritual awareness is an understanding of being imbedded in a larger whole,
a cosmic whole, of belonging to the universe.
— Fritjof Capra

4. I know what the great cure is:
it is to give up, to relinquish, to surrender,
so that our little hearts may beat in unison with the great heart of the world.
— Henry Miller

5. The place to improve the world is first in one's own heart and head and hands.
— Robert M. Pirsig

6. To live is so startling it leaves little time for anything else.
— Emily Dickinson

7. And we should consider every day lost on which we have not danced at least once.
And we should call every truth false which was not accompanied by at least one laugh.
— Friedrich Nietzsche

8. How is one to live a moral and compassionate existence when one is fully aware of the blood, the horror inherent in life, when one finds darkness not only in one's culture but within oneself? If there is a stage at which an individual life becomes truly adult, it must be when one grasps the irony in its unfolding and accepts responsibility for a life lived in the midst of such paradox. One must live in the middle of contradiction, because if all contradiction were eliminated at once life would collapse. There are simply no answers to some of the great pressing questions. You continue to live them out, making your life a worthy expression of leaning into the light.
— Barry Lopez

9. Security is mostly a superstition. It does not exist in nature, nor do the children of men as a whole experience it. Avoiding danger is no safer in the long run than outright exposure. Life is either a daring adventure or nothing.
— Helen Keller

10. One day a boy was watching a holy man praying on the banks of a river in India. When the holy man completed his prayer, the boy went over and asked him, "Will you teach me to pray?" The holy man studied the boy's face carefully. Then he gripped the boy's head in his hands and plunged it forcefully into the water. The boy struggled frantically, trying to free himself in order to breathe. Finally, the holy man released his hold. When the boy was able to get his breath he gasped," What did you do that for?" The holy man said, " I just gave you the first lesson." " What do you mean?" asked the astonished boy. "Well," said the holy man, "when you long to pray as much as you longed to breathe when your head was under water. Only then will I be able to teach you to pray."
— Author Unknown

11. The principle of life is that life responds by corresponding;
your life becomes the thing you have decided it shall be.
— Raymond Charles Barker

12.   A man who becomes conscious of the responsibility he bears toward a human being who affectionately waits for him, or to an unfinished work, will never be able to throw away his life. He knows the "why" for his existence, and will be able to bear almost any "how."
— Victor Frankl

13.   It's not that I'm so smart.
I just stay with the questions much longer.
— Albert Einstein

14.   Whatever is at the center of our life will be the source of our security, guidance, wisdom, and power.
— Stephen Covey

15.   We don't accomplish anything in this world alone ...
and whatever happens is the result of the whole tapestry of one's life
and all the weavings of individual threads
from one to another that creates something.
— Sandra Day O'Connor

16. When you have once seen the glow of happiness on the face of a beloved person,
you know that a man can have no vocation but to awaken that light on the faces surrounding him;
and you are torn by the thought of the unhappiness and night you cast,
by the mere fact of living, in the hearts you encounter.
— Albert Camus

17. A mystic sees beyond the illusion of separateness
into the intricate web of life in which all things are expressions of a single Whole.
You can call this web God, the Tao, the Great Spirit,
the Infinite Mystery, Mother or Father, but it can be known only as Love.
— Joan Borysenko

18.   People say "I want peace."
If you remove I (ego),
and your want (desire),
you are left with peace.
— Satya Sai Baba

19.   Gratitude unlocks the fullness of life.
It turns what we have into enough, and more.
It turns denial into acceptance, chaos to order, confusion to clarity.
It can turn a meal into a feast, a house into a home, a stranger into a friend.
Gratitude makes sense of our past,
brings peace for today,
and creates a vision for tomorrow.
— Melody Beattie

20.   Grant O Lord, that in all the joys of life we may never forget to be kind. Help us to be unselfish in friendship, thoughtful of those less happy than ourselves, and eager to bear the burden of others.
— Charles L. Slattery

21. A moment of love between lovers does not flow like water because everything goes well, but because love teaches them to accept one another with all their frailties. Likewise, our prayer does not flow like water because we succeed in avoiding distractions or falling off to sleep or have reached some altered state of consciousness. Rather, our prayer flows like water insofar as it incarnates our inmost Self surrendered over to the flow of God's self-giving love.
— James Finley

22. My religion consists of a humble admiration of the illimitable superior spirit who reveals himself in the slight details we are able to perceive with our frail and feeble mind.
— Albert Einstein

23. When a man does not know what harbor he is heading for, no wind is the right wind.
— Seneca

24. The master in the art of living makes little distinction between his work and his play, his labor and his leisure, his mind and his body, his information and his recreation,
his love and his religion.
He hardly knows which is which.
He simply pursues his vision of excellence at whatever he does,
leaving others to decide whether he is working or playing.
To him he's always doing both.
 — James A. Michener

25. It is the duty of every cultured man or woman
to read sympathetically the scriptures of the world.
If we are to respect others' religions as we would have them respect our own,
a friendly study of the world's religions is a sacred duty.
— Mohandas K. Gandhi

26. "Tell me the weight of a snowflake," a coal mouse asked a wild dove.

"Nothing more than nothing," was the answer.

"In that case I must tell you a marvelous story," the coal mouse said.

"I sat on a branch of a fir, close to its trunk, when it began to snow, not heavily, not in a giant blizzard, no, just like in a dream, without any violence. Since I didn't have anything better to do, I counted the snowflakes settling on the twigs and needles of my branch. Their number was exactly 3,741,952. When the next snowflake dropped on the branch— nothing more than nothing, as you say, the branch broke off."

Having said that, the coal mouse ran away.

The dove, since Noah's time an authority on the matter, thought about the story for a while and finally said to herself:

"Perhaps there is only one person's voice lacking for peace to come about in the world."

— Kurt Kauter

27.   The capacity for getting along with our neighbor depends to a large extent on the capacity for getting along with ourselves.
The self-respecting individual will try to be as tolerant of his neighbor's shortcomings as he is of his own.
— Eric Hoffer

28.   We must not, in trying to think about how we can make a big difference, ignore the small daily differences we can make which, over time, add up to big differences that we often cannot foresee.
   — Marian Wright Edelman

29.   Our first task in approaching another people, another culture, another religion,
is to take off our shoes, for the place we are approaching is holy.
Else we may find ourselves treading on people's dreams.
More serious still, we may forget that God was here before our arrival.
   — Max Warren

30. Abandon the urge to simplify everything,
to look for formulas and easy answers,
and to begin to think multi-dimensionally,
to glory in the mystery and paradoxes of life,
not to be dismayed by the multitude of causes and consequences that are inherent in each experience — to appreciate the fact that life is complex.
— M. Scott Peck

31. I am the dust in the sunlight, I am the ball of the sun . . .
I am the mist of morning, the breath of evening . . . .
I am the spark in the stone, the gleam of gold in the metal . . . .
The rose and the nightingale, drunk with its fragrance.
I am the chain of being, the circle of the spheres,
The scale of creation, the rise and the fall.
I am what is and is not . . .
I am the soul in all.
— Rumi

FIVE

1. We are members of a vast cosmic orchestra,
in which each living instrument is essential to the complimentary
and harmonious playing of the whole.
— J. Allen Boone

2. The sun, with all those planets revolving around it
and dependent upon it,
can still ripen a bunch of grapes as if it had nothing else
in the universe to do.
— Galileo

3. Because of the interconnectedness of all minds,
affirming a positive vision may be about the most sophisticated action
any one of us can take.
— Willis Harman

4. It is worthwhile to live and fight courageously for sacred ideals.
O blow ye evil winds into my body's fire, my soul you'll never unravel.
Even though disappointed a thousand times or fallen in the fight and everything would worthless seem,
I have lived amidst eternity —
Be grateful, my soul.
My life was worth living.
He who was pressed from all sides but remained victorious in spirit is welcomed into the choir of heroes.
He who overcame the fetters, giving wings to his mind
is entering into the golden age of the victorious.
— Norbert Capek

5. True religion is real living;
living with all one's soul,
with all one's goodness and righteousness.
  — Albert Einstein

6. If everyone gives a thread, the poor man will have a shirt.
— Hindu Proverb

7. We should be careful to get out of an experience
only the wisdom that is in it and stop there;
lest we be like the cat that sits down on a hot stove-lid.
She will never sit down on a hot stove-lid again and that is well;
but also she will never sit down on a cold one anymore.
— Mark Twain

8. The religious community is essential,
for alone our vision is too narrow to see all that must be seen.
Together, our vision widens and strength is renewed.
— Mark Morrison-Reed

9. How does one keep from "growing old inside"?
Surely only in community.
The only way to make friends with time is to stay friends with people….
Taking community seriously not only gives us the companionship we need,
it also relieves us of the notion that we are indispensable.
— Robert McAfee Brown

10. It is impossible for a person to learn what they think they already know.
— Epictetus

11. Why not let people differ about their answers to the great mysteries of the Universe?
Let each seek one's own way to the highest,
to one's own sense of supreme loyalty in life, one's ideal of life.
Let each philosophy, each world-view, bring forth its truth and beauty to a larger perspective,
that people may grow in vision, stature and dedication.
— Algernon Black

12. People may be said to resemble not the bricks of which a house is built, but the pieces of a picture puzzle, each differing in shape, but matching the rest,
and thus bringing out the picture.
— Felix Adler

13. God can only do for you what He can do through you.
— Eric Butterworth

14. We judge ourselves by what we feel capable of doing,
while others judge us by what we have already done.
— Henry Wadsworth Longfellow

15. I once had a sparrow alight upon my shoulder for a moment,
while I was hoeing in a village garden, and I felt that I was more distinguished by that circumstance
that I should have been by any epaulet I could have worn.
— Henry David Thoreau

16. We must be willing to get rid of the life we've planned,
so as to have the life that is waiting for us.
 — Joseph Campbell

17.   Begin doing what you want to do now.
We are not living in eternity.
We have only this moment…
sparkling like a star in our hand-and melting like a snowflake.
— Marie Beyon Ray

18.   We do not grow absolutely, chronologically.
We grow sometimes in one dimension, and not in another; unevenly.
We grow partially. We are relative.
We are mature in one realm, childish in another.
The past, present, and future mingle and pull us backward, forward,
or fix us in the present.
We are made up of layers, cells, constellations.
— Anaïs Nin

19.   One day our descendants will think it incredible
that we paid so much attention to things
like the amount of melanin in our skin
or the shape of our eyes or our gender
instead of the unique identities of each of us
as complex human beings.
— Franklin Thomas

20.   Work when there is work to do.
Rest when you are tired.
One thing done in peace will most likely be better
than ten things done in panic….
I am not a hero if I deny rest;
I am only tired.
— Susan Mc Henry

21.   Only within burns the fire I kindle.
My heart the altar.
My heart the altar.
— poem of a Buddhist Nun

22.   When humans participate in ceremony, they enter a sacred space.
Everything outside of that space shrivels in importance.
Time takes on a different dimension.
Emotions flow more freely.
The bodies of participants become filled with the energy of life,
and this energy reaches out and blesses the creation around them.
All is made new; everything becomes sacred.
— Sun Bear

23.   Besides the noble art of getting things done,
there is the noble art of leaving things undone.
The wisdom of life consists in the elimination of non-essentials.
— Lin Yutang

24.   When one tugs at a single thing in nature,
he finds it attached to the rest of the world.
— John Muir

25.   The same stream of life that runs through my veins night and day
runs through the world and dances in rhythmic measures.
It is the same life that shoots in joy through the dust of the earth
in numberless blades of grass
and breaks into tumultuous waves of leaves and flowers.
It is the same life that is rocked in the ocean-cradle of birth and of death,
in ebb and in flow.
I feel my limbs are made glorious by the touch of this world of life.
And my pride is from the life-throb of ages dancing in my blood this moment.
— Rabindranath Tagore

26.   No snowflake in an avalanche ever feels responsible.
— Voltaire

27. You cannot dream yourself into a character;
you must hammer and forge yourself one.
— James A. Froud

28. "You have been my friend. That in itself is a tremendous thing. I wove my webs for you because I liked you. After all, what's a life, anyway? We're born, we live a little while, we die. A spider's life can't help being something of a mess, with all this trapping and eating flies. By helping you, perhaps I was trying to lift up my life a trifle. Heaven knows anyone's life can stand a little of that."
— "Charlotte" in *Charlotte's Web* by E. B. White

29. You can't shake hands with a clenched fist.
— Indira Gandhi

30. We who lived in concentration camps can remember the men who walked through the huts comforting others, giving away their last piece of bread. They may have been few in number, but they offer sufficient proof that everything can be taken from a man but one thing: the last of the human freedoms — to choose one's attitude in any given set of circumstances, to choose one's own way.
— Viktor Frankl

31. Life is a train of moods like a string of beads;
and as we pass through them they prove to be many colored lenses,
which paint the world their own hue, and each shows us only what lies in its own focus.
— Ralph Waldo Emerson

SIX

1. I would rather have a mind opened by wonder than one closed by belief.
— Gerry Spence

2. Those who are willing to be vulnerable, move among mysteries.
— Theodore Roethke

3. Good character is more to be praised than outstanding talent.
Most talents are, to some extent, a gift.
Good character, by contrast, is not given to us.
We have to build it, piece by piece —
by thought, choice, courage, and determination.
— H. Jackson Brown

4. A man is what he thinks about all day long.
— Ralph Waldo Emerson

5.   At the heart of racism is the religious assertion that God made a creative mistake when God brought some people into being.
— Friedrich Otto Hertz

6.   My desire for knowledge is intermittent; but my desire to commune with the spirit of the universe, to be intoxicated with the fumes, call it, of that divine nectar, to bear my head through atmospheres and over heights unknown to my feet, is perennial and constant."
— Henry David Thoreau

7.   Once upon a time a man whose ax was missing suspected his neighbor's son.
The boy walked like a thief, looked like a thief, and spoke like a thief.
But the man found his ax while digging in the valley, and the next time he saw his neighbor's son, the boy walked, looked and spoke like any other child.
— Lao-Tzu

8. There can be no vulnerability without risk; there can be no community without vulnerability; there can be no peace, and ultimately no life, without community.
— M. Scott Peck

9. We clasp the hands of those that go before us,
and the hands of those who come after us.
We enter the little circle of each other's arms,
And the larger circle of lovers,
Whose hands are joined in a dance,
and the larger circle of all creatures,
Passing in and out of life,
Who move also in a dance,
To a music so subtle and vast that no ear hears it
except in fragments.
— Wendell Berry

10. When you meet someone better than yourself, turn your thoughts to becoming his equal. When you meet someone not as good as you are, look within and examine your own self.
— Confucius

11. Nothing worth doing is completed in our lifetime,
Therefore, we are saved by hope.
Nothing true or beautiful or good makes complete sense
in any immediate context of history;
Therefore, we are saved by faith.
Nothing we do, however virtuous, can be accomplished alone.
Therefore, we are saved by love.
No virtuous act is quite as virtuous from the standpoint of our friend or foe
as from our own;
Therefore, we are saved by the final form of love which is forgiveness.
— Reinhold Neibuhr

12. The notion that we cannot have what we genuinely need is a culturally induced illusion that keeps us mired in the madness of business as usual.
— Parker Palmer

13. An authentic life is the most personal form of worship.
Everyday life has become my prayer.
— Sarah Ban Breathnach

14.   When you have once seen the glow of happiness
on the face of a beloved person,
you know that a man can have no vocation
but to awaken that light on the faces surrounding him;
and you are torn by the thought
of the unhappiness and night you cast,
by the mere fact of living,
in the hearts you encounter.
— Albert Camus

15.   The good we secure for ourselves is precarious and uncertain until it is secured for all of us and incorporated into our common life.
— Jane Addams

16.   In the school of life, difficult people are the faculty. They teach us our most important spiritual lessons, the lessons that we would be most unlikely to learn on our own.
— Mark I. Rosen

17. Start by doing what's necessary; then do what's possible; and suddenly you are doing the impossible.
— St. Francis of Assisi

18. All of us have a supreme jewel in the depth of our hearts,
and we have come into life for no other purpose than to discover this jewel here on earth while we are alive.
— Eknath Easwaran

19. The greatest obstacle to discovery is not ignorance -
it is the illusion of knowledge.
— Daniel J. Boorstin

20. People are asking me about the race problem... I know of no race problem. The great problem that confronts the American people to-day is a national problem — whether this great nation of ours is great enough to live up to its own convictions, carry out its own declaration of independence, and execute the provisions of its own constitution.
— Frederick Douglass

21. I find that principles have no real force except when one is well fed.
— Mark Twain

22. Whenever morality is based on theology,
whenever right is made dependent on divine authority,
the most immoral, unjust, infamous things
can be justified and established.
— Ludwig Feuerbach

23. Everything that irritates us about others can lead us to an understanding of ourselves.
— Carl Jung

24. Be like the bird, who halting in his flight
On limb too slight,
Feels it give way beneath him, yet sings
Knowing he has wings.
— Victor Hugo

25.   One can choose to go back toward safety or forward toward growth.
Growth must be chosen again and again;
fear must be overcome again and again.
— Abraham Maslow

26.   What cannot be achieved in one lifetime will happen when one lifetime is joined to another.
— Harold Kushner

27.   The capacity to love is tied to being able to be awake,
To being able to move out of yourself and be with someone else in a manner that is not about your desire to possess them, but to be with them, to be in union and communion.
— bell hooks

28.   Where there is great love, there are always miracles.
— Willa Cather

29. When I let go of what I am, I become what I might be.
— Lao Tzu

30. The first duty of a human being is to assume
the right functional relationship to society —
more briefly, to find your real job, and do it.
— Charlotte Perkins Gilman

31. It does me no injury for my neighbor to say there are twenty gods or no God.
— Thomas Jefferson

SEVEN

1. The most basic and powerful way to connect to another person is to listen. Just listen. Perhaps the most important thing we ever give each other is our attention… A loving silence often has far more power to heal and to connect than the most well-intentioned words.
— Rachel Naomi Remen

2. I believe that we must doubt our doubt that there is grace. We must open ourselves to the possibility that there are sources beyond ourselves that sustain us, transform us, save us, that hold us tight in the arms of life. I believe that we must open ourselves to the possibility that this grace is already here, that it has been given, is being given, and will be given.
— Rebecca Ann Parker

3. For many, the spiritual is utterly central to all we are and do and say. This is not a mere intellectual understanding.
The authentically spiritual person carries this truth with them even outside the church, into their business life, their family life, their political life and their social life.
— Desmond Tutu

4. Perhaps travel cannot prevent bigotry, but by demonstrating that all peoples cry, laugh, eat, worry, and die, it can introduce the idea that if we try and understand each other, we may even become friends.
— Maya Angelou

5. A rattlesnake, if cornered, will become so angry it will bite itself. That is exactly what the harboring of hate and resentment against others is — a biting of oneself. We think we are harming others in holding these spites and hates, but the deeper harm is to ourselves.
— E. Stanley Jones

6. What we would like to do is change the world…
make it a little simpler for people to feed, clothe, and shelter themselves as God intended them to do. And, by fighting for better conditions, by crying out unceasingly for the rights of the workers, the poor, of the destitute— the rights of the worthy and the unworthy poor, in other words— we can, to a certain extent, change the world; we can work for the oasis, the little cell of joy and peace in a harried world.
We can throw our pebble in the pond and be confident that its ever widening circle will reach around the world.
There is nothing we can do but love, and, dear God, please enlarge our hearts to love each other, to love our neighbor, to love our enemy as our friend.
— Dorothy Day

7. Small is the number of people who see with their eyes and think with their minds.
— Albert Einstein

8. It is often easier to become outraged by injustice half a world away than by oppression and discrimination half a block from home.
— Carl T. Rowan

9. Peace does not fare well where poverty and deprivation reign. It does not flourish where there is ignorance and a lack of education and information. Repression, injustice and exploitation are inimical with peace. Peace is gravely threatened by inter-group fear and envy and by the unleashing of unrealistic expectations. Racial, class and religious intolerance and prejudice are its mortal enemies.
— Frederik W. de Klerk

10. Don't ask yourself what the world needs;
ask yourself what makes you come alive.
And then go and do that.
Because what the world needs is people who have come alive.
— Harold Whitman

11.   The Sufis advise us to speak only after our words have managed to pass through three gates.
At the first gate we ask ourselves, "Are these words true?"
If so, we let them pass on; if not, back they go.
At the second gate we ask, "Are they necessary?"
At the last gate we ask, "Are they kind?
— Eknath Easwaran

12.   I know that you believe that you understood what you think I said,
but I am not sure you realize that what you heard is not what I meant.
— Robert McCloskey

13.   Here is a test to find out whether your mission in life is complete.
If you're alive, It isn't.
 — Richard Bach

14. South African Archbishop Desmond Tutu walked by a construction site on a temporary sidewalk the width of one person. A white man appeared at the other end, recognized Tutu, and said, "I don't make way for gorillas." At which Tutu stepped aside, made a deep sweeping gesture, and said, "Ah, yes, but I do."
— Walter Wink

15. Religion is not about accepting twenty impossible propositions before breakfast,
but about doing things that change you. It is a moral aesthetic, an ethical alchemy.
If you behave in a certain way, you will be transformed.
— Karen Armstrong

16.   One day a young fugitive, trying to hide himself from the enemy, entered a small village. The people were kind to him and offered him a place to stay. But when the soldiers who sought the fugitive asked where he was hiding, everyone became very fearful. The soldiers threatened to burn the village and kill every person unless the young man was handed over to them. The people went to the minister and asked him what to do. Torn between handing over the boy to the enemy and having his people killed, the minister withdrew to his room and read the scriptures, hoping to find an answer. In the early morning, his eyes fell on these words: "It is better that one man dies than the whole people be lost." Then the minister closed his book, called the soldiers, and told them where the boy was hidden. And after the soldiers led the fugitive away to be killed, there was a feast in the village because the minister had saved the lives of the people. But the minister did not celebrate. Overcome with a deep sadness, he remained in his room. That night an angel came to him and asked, "What have you done?" He said: "I handed over the fugitive to the enemy." Then the angel said: "But don't

you know you have handed over the messiah?" "How could I know?" said the minister anxiously. Then the angel said: "If instead of reading the scriptures, you had visited this young man just once and looked into his eyes you would have known."
— Author Unknown

17.   If you think you're too small to have an impact, try going to bed with a mosquito in the room.
— Anita Koddick

18.   If you have come to help me you are wasting your time. But if you recognize that your liberation and mine are bound up together, we can walk together.
— Lila Watson

19.   Our lives begin to end the day we become silent about things that matter.
— Martin Luther King, Jr.

20. It is from numberless diverse acts of courage and belief that human history is shaped. Each time people stand up for an ideal, or act to improve the lot of others, or strike out against injustice, they send forth a tiny ripple of hope, and crossing each other from a million different centers of energy and daring, those ripples build a current that can sweep down the mightiest walls of oppression and resistance.
— Robert F. Kennedy

21. If you want to see the brave,
Look for those who can forgive.
If you want to see the heroic,
Look at those who can love in return for hatred.
— From *The Bhagavad Gita*

22. No matter how big a nation is, it is no stronger than its weakest people, and as long as you keep a person down, some part of you has to be down there to hold him down, so it means you cannot soar as you might otherwise.
— Marian Anderson

23.   People only see what they are prepared to see.
— Ralph Waldo Emerson

24.   You shall know the truth, and the truth shall make you mad.
— Aldous Huxley

25.   I want American history taught. Unless I'm in that book, you're not in it either.
History is not a procession of illustrious people.
It's about what happens to a people.
Millions of anonymous people is what history is about.
— James Baldwin

26.   There is no Middle Ground
If we choose to be on the side of the great Positive Power
we have no choice but to set our hearts and minds
against the destruction around us,
but thought without action is useless.
We must be on one side or the other
and how we will involve ourselves must be the free choice of everyone.
If we choose to act, we must act intelligently and with common sense.
It means we will do everything in our power to understand
the questions we choose to involve ourselves with.
But whatever we are, we must be action people.
Even if the only action possible is to pray.
— Arthur Solomon

27.   We are all affecting the world every moment, whether we mean to or not.
Our actions and states of mind matter, because we are so deeply interconnected with one another.
— Ram Dass

28.　If we remain unable to imagine a world where love can
be recognized as a unifying principle that can lead us to seek and use power wisely,
then we will remain wedded to a culture of domination
that requires us to choose power over love.
— bell hooks

29.　A religious person is one who holds God and humanity in one thought at one time, at all times, who suffers in oneself harms done to others, whose greatest passion is compassion, whose greatest strength is love and defiance of despair.
— Abraham J. Heschel

30. Happiness is the consequence of personal effort. You fight for it, strive for it, insist upon it, and sometimes even travel around the world looking for it. You have to participate relentlessly in the manifestations of your own blessings. And once you have achieved a state of happiness, you must never become lax about maintaining it. You must make a mighty effort to keep swimming upward into that happiness forever, to stay afloat on top of it.
— Elizabeth Gilbert

31. In all our relationships we need to remember the important fact that each person is made to the image and likeness of God. Thus we ought to be able to see reflected in each something of God.
— Basil Hume

EIGHT

1. My definition of a free society is a society where it is safe to be unpopular.
— Adlai Stevens

2. If you want to build a ship, don't herd people together to collect wood and don't assign them tasks and work, but rather teach them to long for the endless immensity of the sea.
— Antoine de Saint-Exupery

3. True religion does not draw men out of the world but enables them to live better in it and excites their endeavors to mend it.
— William Penn

4. Courage doesn't always roar. Sometimes courage is the quiet voice at the end of the day saying, "I will try again tomorrow."
— Mary Ann Radmacher

5. Existence is a strange bargain.
Life owes us little; we owe it everything. The only true happiness comes from squandering ourselves for a purpose.
— Author Unknown

6. You are the embodiment of the information you choose to accept and act upon.
To change your circumstances you need to change your thinking and subsequent actions.
— Adlin Sinclair

7. If you don't know where you are going,
any road will get you there.
— Lewis Carroll

8. If death meant just leaving the stage long enough to change costume and come back as a new character, would you slow down? Or speed up?
— Chuck Palahniuk

9. Learn from yesterday, live for today, hope for tomorrow.
The important thing is to not stop questioning.
— Albert Einstein

10. Be patient toward all that is unsolved in your heart and try to love the questions
themselves, like locked rooms and like books that are now written in a very foreign tongue. Do not now seek the answers, which cannot be given you because you would
not be able to live them. And the point is, to live everything. Live the questions now. Perhaps you will then gradually, without noticing it, live along some distant day into the answer.
— Rainer Maria Rilke

11. To live in this world you must be able to do three things:
to love what is mortal; to hold it against your bones knowing your own life depends on it; and, when the time comes to let it go, to let it go.
— Mary Oliver

12. There are four questions of value in life...
What is sacred?
Of what is the spirit made?
What is worth living for ?
and…. What is worth dying for?
The answer to each is the same.
Only love.
— Johnny Depp

13. The key question to keep asking is, Are you spending your time on the right things?
Because time is all you have.
— Randy Pausch

14. Knowing can be a curse on a person's life. I'd traded in a pack of lies for a pack of truth, and I didn't know which one was heavier. Which one took the most strength to carry around? It was a ridiculous question, though, because once you know the truth, you can't ever go back and pick up your suitcase of lies. Heavier or not, the truth is yours now.
— Sue Monk Kidd

15. Sometimes, when you don't ask questions, it's not because you are afraid that someone will lie to your face. It's because you're afraid they'll tell you the truth.
— Jodi Picoult

16. Happiness is when what you Think, what you Say, and what you Do, are in harmony.
— Mohandas Gandhi

17. Rivers accept things as they are, conform to the shape they find the world in -
Yet nothing changes things more than a river.
Rivers move even mountains into the sea.
— James Dillet Freeman

18. God has placed in each soul an apostle to lead us upon the illumined path.
Yet many seek life from without, unaware that it is within them.
— Kahlil Gibran

19. The Maxim of the Golden Rule does not imply that we should always do to others exactly that which we should wish under our own present circumstances
(which may be quite different from theirs) to be done to us.
What the maxim implies is that we are, as far as possible,
to put ourselves in the place of others; to consider what we would wish to be done to us, were we in their circumstances.
— W.A. Spooner

20. I have ceased to question stars and books;
I have begun to listen to the teaching my blood whispers to me.
— Hermann Hesse

21. If you have an apple and I have an apple and we exchange apples then you and I will still each have one apple.
But if you have an idea and I have an idea and we exchange these ideas, then each of us will have two ideas.
— George Bernard Shaw

22.   Your beliefs become your thoughts,
Your thoughts become your words,
Your words become your actions,
Your actions become your habits,
Your habits become your values,
Your values become your destiny.
— Mohandas Gandhi

23.   The spiritual life is, first of all, a life.
It is not merely something to be known and studied,
it is to be lived.
— Thomas Merton

24.   Freethinkers are those who are willing to use their minds without prejudice and without fearing to understand things that clash with their own customs, privileges, or beliefs. This state of mind is not common, but it is essential for right thinking...
— Leo Tolstoy

25.   Some things have to be believed to be seen.
— Madeleine L'Engle

26. I read and walked for miles at night along the beach, writing bad blank verse and searching endlessly for someone wonderful who would step out of the darkness and change my life. It never crossed my mind that that person could be me.
— Anna Quindlen

27. If the world were merely seductive,
that would be easy.
If it were merely challenging,
that would be no problem.
But I arise in the morning torn between
a desire to improve the world
and a desire to enjoy the world.
This makes it hard to plan the day.
— E.B. White

28. Sometimes our flame goes out,
but is blown again into instant flame by
an encounter with another human being.
— Albert Schweitzer

29. Simplicity, patience, compassion.
These three are your greatest treasures.
Simple in actions and thoughts,
you return to the source of being.
Patient with both friends and enemies,
you accord with the way things are.
Compassionate toward yourself,
you reconcile all beings in the world.
— from the Tao Te Ching

30. We're all made of stories.
When they finally put us underground,
the stories are what will go on.
Not forever, perhaps, but for a time.
It's a kind of immortality, I suppose,
bounded by limits, it's true, but then so
is everything.
— Charles de Lint

31. People are like stained-glass windows.
They sparkle and shine when the sun is out,
but when the darkness sets in,
their true beauty is revealed only if there is a light from within.
— Elisabeth Kűbler-Ross

NINE

1. Communing with God is communing with our own hearts,
our own best selves, not with something foreign and accidental.
Saints and devotees have gone into the wilderness to find God;
of course they took God with them, and the silence and detachment enabled them to hear the still, small voice of their own souls, as one hears the ticking of his own watch in the stillness of the night.
— John Burroughs

2. Spirituality is not to be learned by flight from the world, or by running away from things, or by turning solitary and going apart from the world.
Rather, we must learn an inner solitude wherever or with whomsoever we may be.
We must learn to penetrate things and find God there.
— Meister Eckhart

3. God can be realized through many paths. All religions that teach peace are true. In our human state we are born in the courtyard of the house of God. The important thing is to reach the roof where you can truly see the light. You can reach it by stone stairs or by wooden stairs or by bamboo steps or by a rope. You can also climb up by a bamboo pole. But if you do not aspire to reach the roof you will live your entire life in the courtyard where too many shadows and walls block your view of the sun's pure light.
Go to the roof of your faith, O child of the universe, and bathe in the pureness of the light.
— Ramakrishna

4. You are an aperture through which the universe is looking at and exploring itself
— Alan Wilson Watts

5. Reflection is the lamp of the heart. If it departs, the heart will have no light.
— Imam Al— Haddad

6. Perhaps no one religion contains all of the truth of the world.
Perhaps every religion contains fragments of the truth, and it is our responsibility to identify those fragments and piece them together.
— Christopher Paolini

7. We join spokes together in a wheel,
but it is the center hole
that makes the wagon move.

We shape clay into a pot,
but it is the emptiness inside
that holds whatever we want.

We hammer wood for a house,
but it is the inner space
that makes it livable.

We work with being,
but non-being is what we use.
— Lao-Tzu

8. I believe that imagination is stronger than knowledge. That myth is more potent than history. That dreams are more powerful than facts. That hope always triumphs over experience. That laughter is the only cure for grief. And I believe that love is stronger than death.
— Robert Fulghum

9. The very least you can do in your life is figure out what you hope for.
And the most you can do is live inside that hope.
Not admire it from a distance, but live right in it, under its roof.
— Barbara Kingsolver

10. People say, 'What is the sense of our small effort?'
They cannot see that we must lay one brick at a time, take one step at a time.
A pebble cast into a pond causes ripples that spread in all directions.
Each one of our thoughts, words and deeds is like that.
No one has a right to sit down and feel hopeless.
There's too much work to do.
— Dorothy Day

11. Religion is what an individual does with her solitariness.
— Alfred North Whitehead

12. An Inuit hunter asked the local missionary priest, "If I did not know about God and sin, would I go to hell?" "No," said the priest,
"Not if you did not know."
"Then why," asked the Inuit earnestly, "did you tell me?"
— Annie Dillard

13. The unique personality, which is the real life in me, I cannot gain unless I search for the real life, the spiritual quality, in others. I myself am spiritually dead unless I reach out to the fine quality dormant in others. For it is only with the god enthroned in the innermost shrine of the other, that the god hidden in me, will consent to appear.
— Felix Adler

14. Religion is the human response to being alive and having to die.
— Forrest Church

15.   Everybody prays whether [you think] of it as praying or not. The odd silence you fall into when something very beautiful is happening or something very good or very bad. The ah-h-h-h! that sometimes floats up out of you as out of a Fourth of July crowd when the sky-rocket bursts over the water…The stammer of pain at somebody else's pain…The stammer of joy at somebody else's joy. Whatever words or sounds you use for sighing with over your own life. These are all prayers in their way. These are all spoken not just to yourself but to something even more familiar than yourself and even more strange than the world.
— Frederick Buechner

16.   I prayed for twenty years but received no answer until I prayed with my legs.
— Frederick Douglass

17.   All human beings have an innate need to hear and tell stories and to have a story to live by ... religion, whatever else it has done, has provided one of the main ways of meeting this abiding need.
— Harvey Cox

18.   Dripping water hollows a stone.
— Lucretious

19.   The call to religion is not a call to be better than your fellows,
but to be better than yourself.
Religion is relative to the individual.
— Henry Ward Beecher

20.   If you have knowledge,
let others light their candles at it.
— Margaret Fuller

21.   We are cups, constantly and quietly being filled.
The trick is, knowing how to tip ourselves over and let the beautiful stuff out.
— Ray Bradbury

22. The world is scary because there is always something that has the potential to make you uncomfortable.
If you live your life simply reacting to things you cannot control, then you won't ever be happy with yourself because you don't control your happiness.
Instead, embrace those uncomfortable moments as evidence of your humanity and use them to cherish moments of comfort and love even more.
— Benjamin Wallace

23. Each one of us can make a contribution.
Too frequently we think we have to do spectacular things.
Yet if we remember that the sea is actually made up of drops of water and each drop counts, each one of us can do our little bit where we are.
These little bits can come together and almost overwhelm the world.
Each of us can be an oasis of peace.
— Desmond Tutu

24. Every day I make some gesture, think or feel something through the influence of one or another of these friends….
When I plant bulbs, I pat the earth over each one and realize suddenly that is what my mother did;
I never cook carrots without remembering thyme, a little onion, and sugar as Seline used to do…
These are not conscious evocations nor very important in themselves, but it is their interweaving through every day that explains what influence truly is.
We become what we have loved.
— May Sarton

25. Life is inconvenient, no doubt about it. It's messy.
It is mystery wrapped in an enigma and surrounded by a quandary, all in the shape of a question mark.
It is often more question than answer, more doubt than faith.
It is defined by contradiction, paradox, ambivalence and oxymoron.
That is why human beings invented religion— to figure it all out.
— Richard S. Gilbert

26. I am shocked by the ignorance and wastefulness with which persons who should know better throw away the things they do not like. They throw away experiences, people, marriages, situations, all sorts of things because they do not like them. If you throw away a thing, it is gone. Where you had something you have nothing. Your hands are empty, they have nothing to work on. Whereas, almost all those things which get thrown away are capable of being worked over by a little magic into just the opposite of what they were... But most human beings never remember at all that in almost every bad situation there is the possibility of a transformation by which the undesirable may be changed into the desirable.
— Katherine Butler Hathaway

27. As a single footstep will not make a path on the earth, so a single thought will not make a pathway in the mind. To make a deep physical path, we walk again and again. To make a deep mental path, we must think over and over the kind of thoughts we wish to dominate our lives.
— Henry David Thoreau

28. Beyond our ideas of right-doing and wrong-doing, there is a field.
I'll meet you there.
When the soul lies down in that grass, the world is too full to talk about.
Ideas, language, even the phrase 'each other' doesn't make sense any more.
— Rumi

29. No man treats a motor car as foolishly as he treats another human being.
When the car will not go, he does not attribute its annoying behavior to sin.
He does not say, "You are a wicked motorcar, and I shall not give you any more petrol until you go."
He attempts to find out what is wrong and set it right.
— Bertrand Russell

30. Sometime in your life, hope that you might see one starved man and the look on his face when the bread finally arrives.
Hope that you might have baked it or bought it or even kneaded it yourself.
For that look on his face, for your meeting his eyes across a piece of bread, you might be willing to lose a lot, or suffer a lot, or die a little, even.
— Daniel Berrigan

31. When the Japanese mend broken objects,
they aggrandize the damage by filling the cracks with gold.
They believe that when something's suffered
damage and has a history it becomes more beautiful.
— Barbara Bloom

TEN

1. If all mankind were to disappear, the world would regenerate back to the rich state of equilibrium that existed ten thousand years ago.
If insects were to vanish,
the environment would
collapse into chaos.
— Edward O. Wilson

2. When we come into contact with the other person,
our thoughts and actions should
express our mind of compassion,
even if that person says and does things that are not easy to accept.
We practice in this way until we see clearly that our love is not contingent upon the other person being lovable.
— Thich Nhat Hahn

3. Whatever you have in your mind — forget it;
Whatever you have in your hand —
give it;
Whatever is to be your fate — face it!
— Abu Sa'id

4. Your neighbor is your other-self dwelling behind a wall.
In understanding, all walls shall fall down.
Who knows but that your neighbor is your better-self wearing another body?
See that you love him as you would love yourself.
He too is a manifestation of the Most High.
— Khalil Gibran

5. When one door of happiness closes, another opens;
But often we look so long at the closed door that we do not see the one that has been opened for us.
— Helen Keller

6. No trumpets sound when the important decisions of life are made. Destiny is made known silently.
— Agnes De Mille

7. Everyone must leave something behind when he dies, my grandfather said. A child or a book or a painting or a house or a wall built or a pair of shoes made. Or a garden planted. Something your hand touched some way so your soul has somewhere to go when you die, and when people look at that tree or that flower you planted, you're there.

It doesn't matter what you do, he said, so long as you change something from the way it was before you touched it into something that's like you after you take your hands away. The difference between the man who just cuts lawns and a real gardener is in the touching, he said. The lawn-cutter might just as well not have been there at all; the gardener will be there a lifetime.
— Ray Bradbury

8. We are not going to be able to operate our Spaceship Earth successfully nor for much longer unless we see it as a whole spaceship and our fate as common.
It has to be everybody or nobody.
— R. Buckminster Fuller

9. Cherish your doubts, for doubt is the attendant of truth.
Doubt is the key to the door of knowledge; it is the servant of discovery. A belief which may not be questioned binds us to error, for there is incompleteness and
imperfection in every belief.
Doubt is the touchstone of truth; it is an acid which eats away the false.
Let no one fear for the truth, that doubt may consume it; for doubt is the testing of belief. The truth stands boldly and unafraid; it is not shaken by the testing.
— Robert T. Weston

10. If you are neutral in situations of injustice, you have chosen the side of the oppressor. If an elephant has his foot on the tail of a mouse and you say that you are neutral, the mouse will not appreciate your neutrality.
— Desmond Tutu

11. When I have a terrible need of…shall I say the word…RELIGION…. then I go out and paint the stars.
— Vincent Van Gogh

12.   If you accept that God created everything, you have to accept that She created a universe with a great deal of diversity, with many, many ways of getting the same job done. I can look out my window and see literally hundreds of species of plants, dozens of species of birds, at night you can see big stars, little stars, and so on. Would it make sense, then, that that same God would turn around and say "you can only know me this one way, you must worship with only these sets of words, you must do things this way and no other?"
— Bluejay Adametz

13.   I imagine one of the reasons people cling to their hates so stubbornly is because they sense, once hate is gone, they will be forced to deal with pain.
— James Baldwin

14. A loving person lives in a loving world.
A hostile person lives in a hostile world.
Everyone you meet is your mirror.
— Ken Keyes, Jr.

15. We arrive out of many singular rooms, walking over the branching streets. We come to be assured that brothers and sisters surround us, to restore their images on our eyes. We enlarge our voices in common speaking and singing. We try again that solitude found in the midst of those who with us seek their hidden reckonings. Our eyes reclaim the remembered faces; their voices stir the surrounding air. The warmth of their hands assures us, and the gladness of our spoken names. This is the reason of cities, of homes, of assemblies in the houses of worship. It is good to be with one another.
— Kenneth L. Patton

16.   A young rabbi said to the master, "You know, when I study and when I join others in great feasts, I feel a great sense of light and life. But the minute it's over it's all gone; everything dies in me." The old rabbi replied: "It is just this feeling that happens when a person walks through the woods at night, when the breeze is cool and the scent in the air is delicious. If another joins the traveler with a lantern, they can walk safely and joyfully together. But if they come to a crossroads and the one with the lantern departs then the first must grope her way alone unless she carries her light within her.
— From *Tales of the Hasidim*

17.   If we could read the secret history of our "enemies" we should find in each person's life sorrow and suffering enough to disarm all hostility.
— Henry Wadsworth Longfellow

18. A stream was working itself across the country, experiencing little difficulty. It ran around the rocks and through the mountains. Then it arrived at the desert. Just as it had crossed every other barrier, the stream tried to cross this one. But it found that as fast as it ran into the sand the water disappeared. After many attempts it became very discouraged. It appeared that there was no way it could continue the journey. Then a voice came in the wind. "If you stay the way you are you cannot cross the sands. You cannot become more than a quagmire. To go further, you will have to lose yourself."

"But if I lose myself," the stream cried, "I will never know what I'm supposed to be."

"Oh, on the contrary," said the voice, "if you lose yourself you will become more than you ever dreamed you could be." So the stream surrendered to the dying sun. And the clouds into which it was formed were carried by the raging wind for many miles. Once it crossed the desert, the stream poured down from the skies, fresh and clean and full of energy that comes from storms.

— From the Sufi tradition

19. Life is an adventure in forgiveness
— Norman Cousins

20. Once on the Great Sabbath before the Passover the Rabbi of Roptchitz came home from the house of prayer with weary steps.
"What made you so tired?" asked his wife.
"It was the sermon," he replied.
"I had to speak of the poor and their many needs for the coming Passover. Unleavened bread and wine and everything else is terribly high this year."
"And what did you accomplish with your sermon?" his wife asked.
"Half of what is needed," he answered. "You see, the poor are now ready to take. As for the other half, whether the rich are ready to give— I don't know about that yet."
— from *Tales of the Hasidim*

21. Look back over your life.
What have you consistently done well?
What have you loved to do?
Stand at the intersection of your affections and successes and find your uniqueness.
— Max Lucado

22. A leader takes people where they want to go.
A great leader takes people where they don't necessarily want to go
but ought to be.
— Rosalynn Carter

23. The only difference between saints and sinners is that every saint has a past while every sinner has a future.
— Oscar Wilde

24. A young woman once said to an old woman, what is life's heaviest burden?
And the old woman said, to have nothing to carry.
— from the Jewish tradition

25. I am Peace
Surrounded by Peace
Secure in Peace.
Peace protects me
Peace supports me
Peace is in me
Peace is mine— All is well.
Peace to all beings
Peace among all beings
Peace from all Beings
I am steeped in Peace
Absorbed in Peace
In the streets, at our work,
Having peaceful thoughts,
Peaceful words, peaceful acts.
— from the Buddhist tradition

26. When someone steals another's clothes, we call them a thief. Should we not give the same name to one who could clothe the naked and does not? The bread in your cupboard belongs to the hungry; the coat hanging unused in your closet belongs to the one who needs it; the shoes rotting in your closet belong to the one who has no shoes; the money which you hoard up belongs to the poor.
— Basil the Great

27. …Then I looked over at all those people, all of whom I *detested*, and I saw one layer down, one tiny flick of the lens, I loved them all incredibly. I suddenly saw that the only reason I was angry with them was because I had a model of how I thought it ought to be, which was other than the way it was. How can you get angry at somebody for being what they are?...The next time you get angry, look closely at what you're angry about. You'll see you're angry because God didn't make the world the way *you* think it should have been made. But God makes the world the way she makes it!

…As long as you have certain desires about how it ought to be, you can't see how it is.
— Ram Dass

28. It's easy to make a buck.
It's a lot tougher to make a difference.
— Tom Brokaw

29. Good words will not give my people good health and stop them from dying. Good words will not get my people a home where they can live in peace and take care of themselves.
I am tired of talk that comes to nothing. It makes my heart sick when I remember all the good words and broken promises.
— Chief Joseph

30. To put the world right in order, we must first put the nation in order; to put the nation in order, we must first put the family in order; to put the family in order, we must first cultivate our personal life; we must first set our hearts right.
— Confucius

31. A man's mind may be likened to a garden, which may be intelligently cultivated or allowed to run wild; but whether cultivated or neglected, it must, and will, bring forth. If no useful seeds are put into it, then an abundance of useless weed seeds will fall therein, and will continue to produce their kind. Just as a gardener cultivates his plot, keeping it free from weeds, and growing the flowers and fruits which he requires, so may a man tend the garden of his mind, weeding out all the wrong, useless, and impure thoughts, and cultivating toward perfection the flowers and fruits of right, useful, and pure thoughts, By pursuing this process, a man sooner or later discovers that he is the master gardener of his soul, the director of his life. He also reveals, within himself, the laws of thought, and understands with ever-increasing accuracy, how the thought forces and mind elements operate in the shaping of his character, circumstances, and destiny.
— James Allen

ELEVEN

1. By three methods we may learn wisdom:
First, by reflection, which is noblest;
Second, by imitation, which is easiest;
and Third by experience, which is the bitterest.
— Confucius

2. When you do the common things in life in an uncommon way,
you will command the attention of the world.
— George Washington Carver

3. There is an endless net of threads throughout the universe…
At every crossing of the threads there is an individual.
At every individual is a crystal bead.
And every crystal bead reflects.
Not only the light from every other crystal in the net
But also every other reflection throughout the entire universe.
— Anne Adams

4. All of the places in our lives are sanctuaries;
some of them just happen to have steeples.
And all of the people in our lives are saints;
it is just that some of them have day jobs
and most will never have feast days named for them.
— Robert Benson

5. Begin doing what you want to do now.
We are not living in eternity.
We have only this moment, sparkling like a star in our hand—
and melting like a snowflake.
— M.B. Ray

6. God is good, but never dance in a small boat.
— From the Irish tradition

7. In life a person can be a builder or a planter.
Builders may spend years on their task but one day they will finish.
Then, hemmed in by their own walls- life becomes meaningless once the building is finished.
Planters suffer the storms and seasons and rarely stop,
for a garden never stops growing
and by its constant demands on the gardener's attentions,
it makes of the gardener's life a great adventure.
— Paul Coehlo

8. Only at that shrine where all are welcome will God sing loud enough to be heard.
— Theresa of Avila

9. May I have the courage today
To live the life that I would love
To postpone my dream no longer
But do at last what I came here for
And waste my heart on fear no more.
— John O' Donohue

10. There are beautiful wild forces within us.
Let them turn the mills inside and fill sacks
That feed even heaven.
— Francis of Assisi

11. Success is not defined by position or pay scale but by this:
Doing the most what you do the best.
— Max Lucado

12. The last quality I would like to mention is modesty:
the ability to see that the openings possible to us are limited,
that none of us is in a position to change the whole world,
to change the entire structure of our society,
but that we are able to do a certain limited amount.
Our danger is that by dreaming to change the whole thing
we are not available to do the limited thing which is possible for us.
— Thomas Cullinan

13. Before you tell your life what you intend to do with it, listen for what it intends to do with you. Before you tell your life what truths and values you decided to live up to, let your life tell you what truths you embody, what values you represent.
— Parker Palmer

14. Religion is what men and women in community do, say, and think, in that order, with respect to those things, real or imagined, over which they have no control.
— Arthur Darby Nock

15. Only if a person truly belongs to a community, naturally and unselfconsciously, can one enter into the living stream and lead a full, creative, spontaneous life, at home in the world and at one with self and one's fellows, enjoying a recognized status, and thereby acquiring a vision of life…free from the crippling wounds inflicted by the real or imaginary superiority of others.
— Isaiah Berlin

16. The more faithfully you listen to the voice within you, the better you will hear what is sounding outside. And only he who listens can speak. Is this the starting point of the road towards the union of your two dreams — to be allowed in clarity of mind to mirror life and in purity of heart to mold it?
— Dag Hammarskjold

17. To act choicelessly is to act in accord with the situation.
If someone throws a rock, you duck.
— Rami Shapiro

18. Prayer is not asking.
It is a longing of the soul.
It is a daily admission of one's weakness….
And so, it is better in prayer to have a heart without words
than words without a heart.
— Gandhi

19. We have to live today by what truth we can get today and be ready tomorrow to call it falsehood.
— William James

20. A simpler life-style is not a panacea. It may be embarked upon for the wrong reasons- out of guilt, as a substitute for political action, or in quest for moral "purity." But it can also be meaningful and significant:
— as an act of faith performed for the sake of personal integrity and as an expression of a personal commitment to a more equitable distribution of the world's wealth;
— as an act of self-defense against the mind-polluting effects of our overconsumption;
— as an act of solidarity with the majority of humankind,
which has no choice about life-style;
— as an act of celebration of the riches found in creativity, spirituality, and community with others, rather than in mindless materialism.
— Thomas G. Pettepiece

21. God grant me the serenity to accept the people I cannot change, the courage to change the one I can, and the wisdom to know it's me.
— Author unknown

22. The biggest problem in the world could have been solved when it was small.
— Witter Bynner

23. Never make your home in a place. Make a home for yourself inside your own head. You'll find what you need to furnish it: memory, friends you can trust, love of learning, and other such things. That way it will go with you wherever you journey.
— Tad Williams

24. Serve God with all your might while the candle is burning, and then when it goes out for a season, you will have the less to regret.
— Charles H. Spurgeon

25. You can never get enough of what you don't need to make you happy.
— Eric Hoffer

26. The paradox of hospitality is that it wants to create emptiness, but a friendly emptiness where strangers can enter and discover themselves as created free; free to sing their own songs, speak their own languages, dance their own dances; free also to leave and follow their own vocations. Hospitality is not a subtle invitation to adopt the lifestyle of the host, but the gift of a chance for the guest to find his own.
— Henri J. M .Nouwen

27. It is impossible to pray to a personal God — that is, love a personal God- and remain indifferent to those who are suffering.
It is impossible.
Anyone who prays without suffering for his or her suffering brothers and sisters is praying to a pole, a shadow, not the living God.
— Carlo Carretto

28. He hoped and prayed that there wasn't an afterlife. Then he realized there was a contradiction involved here and merely hoped that there wasn't an afterlife.
— Douglas Adams

29. There is no need for temples, no need for complicated philosophies. My brain and my heart are my temples; my philosophy is kindness.
— The Dalai Lama

30. You can safely assume that you've created God in your own image when it turns out that God hates all the same people you do.
— Anne Lamott

31. We search for happiness everywhere, but we are like Tolstoy's fabled beggar who spent his life sitting on a pot of gold, under him the whole time. Your treasure--your perfection--is within you already. But to claim it, you must leave the busy commotion of the mind and abandon the desires of the ego and enter into the silence of the heart.
— Elizabeth Gilbert

TWELVE

1. Do not go where the path may lead. Go instead where there is no path and leave a trail.
— Ralph Waldo Emerson

2. Every person is a damn fool for at least five minutes every day; wisdom consists in not exceeding the limit.
— Elbert Hubbard

3. The dedicated community is formed, shaken up, and formed anew when we discover our personal story within earlier stories of our heritage. When we permit our story to grow within the embrace of our common story, we strengthen one another. Then we take risks to realize a shared vision of justice and peace that we never would have taken alone.
— George Kimmich Beach

4. Please remember,
it is what you are that heals,
not what you know.
— Carl Jung

5. The glory of friendship is not the outstretched hand,
nor the kindly smile, nor the joy of companionship;
it is the spiritual inspiration that comes to one when he discovers that someone else believes in him and is willing to trust him with his friendship.
— Ralph Waldo Emerson

6. Lead me from death to life,
From falsehood to truth.
Lead me from despair to hope,
From fear to trust.
Lead me from hate to love,
From war to peace.
Let peace fill my heart,
my world, my universe.
Amen
— Universal Peace Prayer

7. For you, there is only one road that can lead to God and this is fidelity,
to remain constantly true to yourself, to what you feel is highest in you.
— P. Teilhard de Chardin

8. Four things never come back to us - the spoken word, the sped arrow, time past, and the neglected opportunity.
— Author Unknown

9. There's a lovely Hasidic story of a rabbi who always told his people that if they studied the Torah, it would put Scripture on their hearts. One of them asked, "Why on our hearts, and not in them?" The rabbi answered, "Only God can put Scripture inside. But reading sacred text can put it on your heart, and then when your hearts break, the holy words will fall inside.
— Anne Lamott

10. People may be said to resemble not the bricks of which a house is built, but the pieces of a picture puzzle, each differing in shape, but matching the rest, and thus bringing out the picture.
— Felix Adler

11.   There's a trick to the "graceful exit." It begins with the vision to recognize when a job, a life stage, or a relationship is over — and let it go. It means leaving what's over without denying its validity or its past importance to our lives. It involves a sense of future, a belief that every exit line is an entry, that we are moving up, rather than out.
— Ellen Goodman

12.   People who fail at life
excuse their faults;
people who succeed
abandon them.
— From the Hindu tradition

13. One of the few people I know who behaves sensibly is my tailor;
he takes my measurements anew each time he sees me.
Most others go on with their old measurements
and expect me to fit them,
as if I should not grow or change as I move through life.
— George Bernard Shaw

14. There is only one history of any importance,
and it is the history of what you once believed in,
and the history of what you came to believe in.
— Kay Boyle

15. The shortest distance between truth and a human being is a story.
— Anthony de Mello

16. Help your brother's boat across and your own will reach the shore.
— from the Hindu tradition

17. Miracles do not happen in contradiction to nature,
but only in contradiction to that which is known to us in nature.
— St. Augustine

18. Anyone who expects to do good must not expect
people to roll stones out of his way but must
accept his lot calmly even if they roll a few more into it.
— Albert Schweitzer

19. An eye for an eye makes the whole world blind.
— Gandhi

20. Action is what separates a belief from an opinion.
— Ibu Patel

21. Sow an action and reap a habit;
sow a habit and reap a character;
sow a character and reap a destiny.
— Ralph Waldo Emerson

22. Considerable evidence suggests that if we use an increase in our incomes, as many of us do, simply to buy bigger houses and more expensive cars, then we do not end up any happier than before. But if we use an increase in our incomes to buy more of certain inconspicuous goods — such as freedom from a long commute or a stressful job — then the evidence paints a very different picture. The less we spend on conspicuous consumption goods, the better we can afford to alleviate congestion; and the more time we can devote to family and friends, to exercise, sleep, travel, and other restorative activities. On the best available evidence, reallocating our time and money in these and similar ways would result in healthier, longer — and happier — lives.
— Robert H. Frank

23. You cannot find yourself, only create yourself.
— Anne B. Sekel

24. Silence is the beautiful fruit of prayer.
We must learn not only the silence of the mouth,
but also the silence of the heart, of the eyes, of the ears and of the mind,
which I call the five silences.
Say it and memorize it on your five fingers.
— Mother Teresa

25. When the body sinks into death, the essence of man is revealed. Man is a knot, a web, a mesh into which relationships are tied. Only those relationships matter. The body is an old crock that nobody will miss. I have never known a man to think of himself when dying. Never.
— Antoine de Saint-Exupery

26.   Don't let the noise of others' opinions drown out your own inner voice. And most important, have the courage to follow your own heart and intuition. They somehow already know what you truly want to become. Everything else is secondary.
— Steve Jobs

27.   If you've lost your life's true passion (or if you're struggling desperately to find passion in the first place), don't sweat it. Back off for a while. But don't go idle, either. Just try something different, something you don't care about so much. Why not try following mere curiosity, with its humble, roundabout magic? At the very least, it will keep you pleasantly distracted while life sorts itself out. At the very most, your curiosity may surprise you. Before you even realize what's happening, it may have led you safely all the way home.
— Elizabeth Gilbert

28. The end comes when we no longer talk with ourselves. It is the end of genuine thinking and the beginning of the final loneliness.
The remarkable thing is that the cessation of the inner dialogue marks also the end of our concern with the world around us. It is as if we noted the world and think about it only when we have to report it to ourselves.
— Eric Hoffer

29. Your work is to discover your work and then to give yourself to it with all your heart.
— From *The Dhammapada*

30. In theory there is no difference between theory and practice. In practice there is.
— Yogi Berra

31. The most beautiful and most profound emotion we can experience is the sensation of the mysterious. It is the fundamental emotion that stands at the cradle of true art and true science. He who knows it not and can no longer wonder, no longer feel amazement, is as good as dead, a snuffed-out candle. To know that what is impenetrable to us really exists, manifesting itself as the highest and the most radiant beauty which our dull faculties can comprehend only in their most elementary forms — this knowledge, this feeling, is at the center of true religiousness. What is the meaning of human life, or of organic life altogether? To answer this question at all implies a religion. Is there any sense then, you ask, in putting it? I answer, the man who regards his own life, and that of his fellow-creatures, as meaningless is not merely unfortunate but almost disqualified for life.
— Albert Einstein

THE RETREATS

Retreat Template:
Arrival Ritual   (Introductions, check in, leave baggage, schedule etc.)
Candle Lighting and Centering
Readings
Listening
Reflection
Silence
Closing Ritual
Closing Readings
Departure

Retreat Themes:
One: Openness
Two: Hospitality
Three: Connection
Four: Imagination
Five: Gratitude
Six: Silence
Seven: Wonder
Eight: Play
Nine: Shadow
Ten: Mindfulness
Eleven: Listening
Twelve: Justice

RETREAT ONE - OPENNESS

Practicing openness means trying to live with an open heart, an open attitude of acceptance, and a certain amount of risk taking. It means trying to get rid of preconceived notions and embrace possibilities— even to be uncomfortable sometimes. It is sometimes messy. It means being receptive to new ideas. It means not always being in control and allowing others and other things to be in the spotlight as teachers and guides. It is a way of living that allows us to use our whole selves to experience what life has to offer.

What areas of my life would benefit from being more wholly open to life?

Arrival

If you are retreating alone - use this time to unencumber: turn off phones, acquaint yourself with the space and set up the space the way you will want it for the day, unpack supplies.

If you are retreating in a group, use this time to unencumber as described above PLUS:
Give everyone the opportunity to introduce themselves if appropriate, tell a little about their life at present, and also tell what items they are putting away for the day so they will be able to be as present as possible during the retreat.

Candle Lighting and Readings
Light a candle and choose several passages to read aloud from the following list as a way to center everyone's attention on the retreat theme.

a. Open yourself to the Tao- the Way, then trust your natural responses
and watch everything fall into place.
— The Tao Te Ching

b. If your everyday practice is open to all your emotions, to all the people you meet, to all the situations you encounter,

without closing down, trusting that you can do that - then that will take you as far as you can go. And then you'll understand all the teachings that anyone has ever taught.
— Pema Chodron

c. May my feet rest firmly on the ground
May my head touch the sky
May I see clearly
May I have the capacity of listen
May I be free to touch
May my words be true
May my heart and mind be open
May my hands be empty to fill the need
May my arms be open to others
May my gifts be revealed to me
So that I may return that
which has been given
Completing the great circle.
— Terma Collective

d. I would define love very simply: as a potent blend of openness and warmth, which allows us to make real contact, to take delight in and appreciate, and to be at one with— — our selves, others, and

life itself. Openness— — the heart's pure, unconditional yes— — is love's *essence*. And warmth is love's basic *expression*, arising as a natural extension of this yes— — the desire to reach out and touch, connect with, and nourish what we love.
— John Welwood

e.   Don't be afraid of messiness.
Isn't the sun messy with its love?
Doesn't rain bring life and spoilage with one sleek stroke?
Can't beauty sometimes disguise itself as bruises?
Isn't a piece of dust allowed to sing?
Happiness already knows we often forget to unwrap it.
It just lies quietly, a dazzling seed inching upward in our hard ground, waiting for our eyes
to become Spring.
— Elsa Joy Bailey

f.   *Rumi's Awakened Heart*

One day Rumi asked one of his young, snotty disciples to give him an enormous amount of rich and delicious food. This young disciple was rather alarmed because he thought Rumi was living an ascetic lifestyle. Rumi used to pray all night and eat hardly anything. The disciple thought, "Aha, now I've really got the master — what he really wants to do is to go off somewhere secretly and eat all this food!" So he decided to follow Rumi. He followed him through the streets of Konya, out into the fields, out into yet further fields. Then he saw Rumi go into a ruined tomb. "I'm finally going to unmask his pretensions," the young disciple thought. But what he found was a totally exhausted bitch with six puppies, and Rumi was feeding the dog with his own hands so that she could survive to feed her children. Rumi knew that the disciple was following him, of course, and turned to him smiling and said, "See?" The disciple, extremely moved, said, "But how on earth did you know that she was here? How did you know that she was hungry? This is miles away from where you are!" Rumi laughed and laughed, "When you have become awake your ears are so acute that they can hear the

cries of a sparrow ten thousand miles away."
— from *The Way of Passion: A Celebration of Rumi* by Andrew Harvey

g. The Open Heart
"When the heart opens, we forget ourselves and the world pours in: this world and also the invisible world of meaning that sustains everything that was and ever shall be. When the heart opens, everything matters, and this world and the next become one and the same."
— from *Ten Poems to Open Your Heart* by Roger Housden

Listening
Allow some time, 30 minutes or more, for each person to go off on his or her own and process the opening readings. The readings can be written on a large piece of paper for participants to refer to or they can be printed on slips of paper for each person. This time allows for the processing of the words within the hearts and minds of each individual.

Participants may want to sit/walk with the readings and then journal about their relationship to the readings and any other insights they notice during this time, or they may want to use their journals as a place in which to have a conversation with themselves and/or the Divine on the topic.

___

Reflection
"Hearts need education and refinement just as the body needs exercise and moderation." Kabir Helminski, a Sufi sheikh

The activities in this section are intended to give retreat participants the opportunity to have a relationship with the retreat theme...to reflect, to re-create, co-create themselves in the light of their experiences. This can be done in many ways but the ultimate goal is to open oneself to the theme and find ways to incorporate the messages from the listening session into one's being. Participants may want to choose just one activity and spend the allotted time on that one pursuit or they may want to choose a couple of things to spend their time on. Groups may choose to all do the same thing for a time and then come back together to discuss the activity.

A. Walking Meditation
In case it isn't obvious, this kind of meditation is done with the eyes open. Choose a place to walk that is away from traffic and on a level surface so that you can walk without paying too much attention to obstacles. You might begin with a 20-minute walk, although it is up to you how long you walk. It all depends on how much time you have. The purpose of this kind of meditation is to develop a greater awareness and a greater understanding of yourself in your ordinary life. This kind of practice is something that can be done on a short walk through a parking lot or on a wooded trail during a lunch break.

As you begin, simply stand in place and feel your feet on the earth. Feel the way your feet balance your body on the ground. As you begin to walk, walk at a slow but normal pace. Be aware of your foot as the heel makes contact with the ground first and then as your foot rolls forward onto the ball, and then as it lifts and travels through the air. Be aware of how your foot feels in your shoe, of your ankles and how relaxed they are, of your calves and knees and thighs as you walk.

Follow your awareness up your body to your neck and then, eventually, to the top of your head, relaxing all of those parts as you continue to walk. Notice your jaw especially…is it relaxed? If not, try to relax it.

Are you bored or content or agitated? Are you feeling happy or sad? Notice your emotions. Is your mind busy, or is it calm? Are you thinking about things unconnected with this practice? For now, just notice these things with no particular judgment.

Next, slowly but purposefully, breathe in and out and repeat one of the following mantras as you walk:
- Open my eyes that I may see
- May I be open to life
- May I be open to possibilities

- Open, open, open….

Continue your walk for as long as you have allotted for this practice. You may want to journal about this experience or discuss it with others who are on retreat with you.

B. The Heart at Your Center

Visualize your heart, beating in the center of your chest.

Take a mental picture of that heart.

What is the purpose of your heart…literally, spiritually, metaphorically?

Have a conversation with you heart.

What does it say to you?
Draw your heart.

C. Open Stretches

Find an outdoor or indoor space where you have room to stretch your arms open wide without running into anything or having anyone else in your space or you in theirs. Spend some time standing, or sitting if you cannot stand, with your arms stretched out and open wide. Listen to what your life is telling you as you open yourself to its message.

Optional: Use one of the following mantras as you stretch:

- Open my eyes that I may see
- May I be open to life
- May I be open to possibilities
- Open, open, open….

D. "Open" Collage

Create a collage out of paper, pictures from magazines etc., natural items….that helps you to visually explore what it means to be open. Use one of the quotes from section B: Journaling Themes, above if you need a focus. Share your collage with others on the retreat with you after you have finished.

Gather supplies: magazines, found objects, photos, drawings etc. cardboard, wood or other sturdy object to glue the collage pieces onto, glue stick or rubber cement.

Create collage: by positioning cut out or torn pieces of pa per onto the cardboard backing to make a unified design. You may want to put a few pieces in place and play with their position before permanently affixing them.

Finishing: after your collage is complete, spray with a shellac to seal or use Mod-Podge sealer. Brush a thin layer of the Mod-Podge over the entire collage using a foam craft brush and then let dry. The Mod-Podge dries clear.

Silence
Spend some time (15-20 minutes minimum) sitting or walking in silence as a way to process the activities and messages of the day.

Closing Ritual

As the retreat comes to a close, choose one of the following ways to process your exploration of openness.

If you are on an individual retreat, spend some time reflecting on the retreat in your journal. It may be helpful to use some of the following questions:

- What did I learn about myself today that I did not know or acknowledge before I arrived?
- How will I practice openness in my daily life?
- Has taking time away from my routine life and retreating helped me to know myself in a deeper way? What have I learned?
- What does being "open" mean to me?

If you are on a group retreat, gather the group together to engage in a closing ritual to help them process the lessons of the day and to say goodbye to the others they shared the experience with. You may want to choose one of the following rituals to engage in as a way to process the retreat.

- Invite participants to come forward, one at a time, light a candle, (or choose a stone or shell from the basket provided and drop the stone into a shallow bowl of water) and tell the group what they have learned about themselves today OR tell what value today's retreat has had for them.

- Give each participant a square of aluminum foil (or white Model Magic or Play-Doh) and ask them to create a symbol of the soul work they have done on this retreat. After giving the group sufficient time to create their symbol, go around the circle and ask each person to tell about their symbol. Place the symbols on a table in the middle of the circle and leave them there during the closing reading.

- Write a poem or prayer as a group as a way to end your time together. Ask each person to come up with a word or phrase that describes the value they have found in being together today or what they have learned about themselves during this time. Each person then writes the word or phrase on a large piece of easel paper. All the phrases are written together on the same large piece of paper. After all have had a chance to contribute, read the poem/prayer aloud together as a group.

- Create a web prayer using a large ball of yarn. Have the group stand in a circle. The person with the ball of yarn wraps a foot or two of the yarn loosely around his or her wrist and then says aloud a word or phrase that tells something about what they have learned about themselves today in relation to the theme of the retreat. When they are finished they unroll a few yards of the yarn and gently toss the ball to someone across from them while continuing to hold on to their piece of yarn. The thrower may want to make eye contact with the intended recipient or even tell them they are going to throw the ball to them so they will be ready. The recipient catches the ball and repeats the process. The ritual continues in this way until all have had a turn. When the activity is finished a web of connection is visible as the yarn criss-crosses from person to person.

Closing Readings

Choose one of the following readings to close your time together, after which participants can make plans for their departure.

Turning to One Another
by Meg Wheatley

There is no power greater than a community discovering what it cares about.
Ask: "What's possible?" not "What's wrong?" Keep asking.
Notice what you care about.
Assume that many others share your dreams.
Be brave enough to start a conversation that matters.
Talk to people you know.
Talk to people you don't know.
Talk to people you never talk to.

Be intrigued by the differences you hear. Expect to be surprised.
Treasure curiosity more than certainty.
Invite in everybody who cares to work on what's possible.
Acknowledge that everyone is an expert about something.
Know that creative solutions come from new connections.
Remember, you don't fear people whose story you know.
Real listening always brings people closer together.
Trust that meaningful conversations can change your world.
Rely on human goodness.
Stay together.

Go in Peace and Live with Intention   by Ben Wallace

Each of us has a power within us. We have brought with us gifts and talents, experiences and dreams. As we leave here, know that we are more powerful because of the parts of us that we have shared with each other. Take these gifts and dreams and go out into the world to share that power with others. Know that inspiring others starts with finding the inspiration inside ourselves. We cannot pass our fire to others without taking time to kindle and stoke those fires within ourselves. May this time have served to help each of us tend to our own fires so that we may share that light and warmth with the rest of the world. Go in peace and live with intention.

From the Buddhist Tradition

May I become at all times, both now and forever
A protector for those without protection
A guide for those who have lost their way
A ship for those with oceans to cross
A bridge for those with rivers to cross
A sanctuary for those in danger
A lamp for those without light

A place of refuge for those who lack shelter
And a servant to all in need.

Go In Peace
by Mark L. Belletini

Go in peace. Live simply, gently, at home in yourselves.
Act justly.
Speak justly.
Remember the depth of your own compassion.
Forget not your power in the days of your powerlessness.
Do not desire to be wealthier than your peers
And stint not your hand of charity.
Practice forbearance.
Speak the truth, or speak not.
Take care of yourselves as bodies,
For you are a good gift.
Crave peace for all people in the world,
Beginning with yourselves
And go as you go with the dream
Of that peace alive in your heart.

Great Gaia
by Ben Stallings

Great Gaia,
living spirit of the Earth:
Thank you for this beautiful day.
Thank you for the ground we
walk on, which is your body.
Thank you for the water we drink,
which is your blood.
Thank you for the air we breathe,
which is your breath.
Thank you for the community of
life that surrounds us and
sustains us;
this is your living pulse.
Thank you for the kind thoughts
of friends and strangers; these
are your thoughts.
Thank you for this beautiful day.

Go in Peace and Compassion
by Ben Wallace
Each of us is richer because of
the time we have shared here
together. That richness comes

from the gifts we have shared
with each other, gifts that change
us for the better. Let us now
share a moment of silence
together, focusing within
ourselves and recognizing the
gifts that we have been given.
(Pause for a moment) Now let us
go out into the world and share
our gifts in order to inspire that
future which we hope to live in.
Go in peace and compassion.

By Rabbi Mordecai M. Kaplan

Don't merely expect to find or to
believe that life is worthwhile;
make it worthwhile. Don't merely
see life whole; make it whole.
Not knowing which should come
first, to improve one's self or to
improve the world, we end up
doing neither.
Actually, the only way to improve
the world is by improving one's
self, and the only way to improve
one's self is by improving the
world.

Building the Dream
  by Maria Wilson

Group 1: We journey together
  Searching forever
  Think of what we'll do.
  Something amazing
  Something courageous
  Together we'll make our dreams come true.
Group 2: We've got potential
  Faith evidential
  Together we'll live without any fear.
  Won't be defeated
  Won't be divided
  Building the dream we've made to share.
  All: Find your dream
  Live your dream
  Stand up for your dream
  We're building the dream
Group 1: Justice and action
  No dissatisfaction
  Encourage all who come your way.
  Your spirit will flourish

　　　　　All souls we will nourish
　　　　　Together we learn and play.
Group 2: Love, inspiration,
　　　　　Communication,
　　　　　Building our world with love and care.
　　　　　Accepting, embracing,
　　　　　Thoughts set my heart racing
　　　　　Building the dream, I'll see you there.
　　All: Be who you are, be inspired.
　　　　　Be at peace.
　　　　　Bring all you love.
　　　　　Share your joy, share your grief,
　　　　　Come let your soul find relief.

Departure

RETREAT TWO - HOSPITALITY

Practicing hospitality means welcoming the stranger as a holy guest. It means welcoming the Divine in the body of a stranger. Being a person who practices hospitality means living your life as though every day were an 'open house'. It means dismantling the barriers to welcome in our daily lives and creating a world where people choose to become a friend instead of remaining a stranger. What barriers have I erected for safety and out of fear that I might consider dismantling in order to practice hospitality?

Arrival

If you are retreating alone - use this time to unencumber: turn off phones, acquaint yourself with the space and set up the space the way you will want it for the day, unpack supplies.

If you are retreating in a group, use this time to unencumber as described above PLUS:
Give everyone the opportunity to introduce themselves if appropriate, tell a little about their life at present, and also tell what items they are putting away for the day so they will be able to be as present as possible during the retreat.

Candle Lighting and Readings
Light a candle and choose several passages to read aloud from the following list as a way to center everyone's attention on the retreat theme.

a. Let me live in my house by the side of the road,
Where the race of men go by;
They are good, they are bad;
they are weak, they are strong,
Wise, foolish — so am I;
Then why should I sit in the scorner's seat,
Or hurl the cynic's ban?

Let me live in my house by the side of the road,
And be a friend to man.
— Sam Walter Foss

b. When I am a good host, I can order the world precisely as I believe it ought to be. It is a world that I have created in my mind and in my own image, and it gladdens me profoundly to see it unfold without original sin, without expulsions and floods and disobedience and illness. When I am a good guest, I have returned to Eden, where everything I need is provided for me, including companionship and a benevolent deity at my shoulder serving me and protecting me. The concept of paradise may be backward-looking but the concept of heaven is anticipatory. Perhaps this is what heaven will be like? A great table of oak worn smooth with age and candle wax; a dimly lit room, a quartet of angels playing Sarah Vaughan in the corner; this blissful throb of quiet, intelligent conversation; bubbling pots and aromatic stews that no one seems to have worked to prepare; and you - you have nothing to worry about, not now, not here, not for

all eternity. Leave it all behind at the threshold, forget everything, for here in heaven, you are my guest.
— Jesse Browner

c. True hospitality is marked by an open response to the dignity of each and every person. Henri Nouwen has described it as receiving the stranger on his own terms, and asserts that it can be offered only by those who "have found the center of their lives in their own hearts."
— Kathleen Norris

d. There is no beautifier of complexion, or form, or behavior, like the wish to scatter joy and not pain around us. 'Tis good to give a stranger a meal, or a night's lodging. 'Tis better to be hospitable to his good meaning and thought, and give courage to a companion. We must be as courteous to a man as we are to a picture, which we are willing to give the advantage of a good light.
— Ralph Waldo Emerson

e. In her book, *The Lady in the Palazzo,* Marlena De Blasi says, "It's not what's on the table, but who's on the chairs." Don't misunderstand; food and hospitality are intimately related, but sometimes we need to adjust our priorities. Great cooks and not-so-great cooks often share the same problem: pride and ego and can get in the way of connecting with others. And isn't connecting what it's all about?
— Susan Ely
(http://thesharedtable.com)

f. I hear these words about "the poor"
and brush them into the corners of my mind.
I cannot think about them now
I am too preoccupied
with the choice of hors d'oeuvres for my party
and the color of my new shoes.
I am too anxious
about the impression I make
to decide for diminishing
or to question the givens.
I am too cautious
to risk the highway
that leads away from safe places.
Convenience blankets me,

stifles the clamor of a hungry world.
— Sara Covin Juengst in *Breaking Bread, the Spiritual Significance of Food.*

g. When we speak of hospitality we are always addressing issues of inclusion and exclusion. Each of us makes choices about who will and who will not be included in our lives…. Hospitality has an inescapable moral dimension to it…. All of our talk about hospitable openness doesn't mean anything as long as some people continue to be tossed aside…. But calling hospitality a moral issue does not tell us the whole truth about hospitality either. A moral issue can become bogged down in legalisms, and hospitality is no legalistic ethical issue. It is instead a spiritual practice, a way of becoming more human, a way of understanding yourself. Hospitality is both the answer to modern alienation and injustice and a path to a deeper spirituality.
— Father Daniel Homan and Lonni Gollins Pratt *in Radical Hospitality: Benedict's Way of Love*

Listening

Allow some time, 30 minutes or more, for each person to go off on their own and process the opening readings. The readings can be written on a large piece of paper for participants to refer to or they can be printed on slips of paper for each person. This time allows for the processing of the words within the hearts and minds of each individual. Participants may want to sit/walk with the readings and then journal about their relationship to the readings and any other insights they notice during this time, or they may want to use their journals as a place in which to have a conversation with themselves and/or the Divine on the topic.

Reflection

"Hearts need education and refinement just as the body needs exercise and moderation." Kabir Helminski, a Sufi sheikh

The activities in this section are intended to give retreat participants the opportunity to have a relationship with the retreat theme...to reflect, to re-create, co-create themselves in the light of their experiences. This can be done in many ways but the ultimate goal is to open oneself to the theme and find ways to incorporate the messages from the listening session into one's being. Participants may want to choose just one activity and spend the allotted time on that one pursuit or they may want to choose a couple of things to spend their time on. Groups may choose to all do the same thing for a time and then come back together to discuss the activity.

A. Small Group Discussion Questions

1. The Key to Hospitality
"A tavola, non si invecchia."
"At the table, you don't grow old," declared my first year Italian instructor. Maybe that was true in Italy — but not at my house. My intentions were good, but by the time I'd finally get the food on the table, I felt older than the aged cheese on the antipasto tray. I loved

cooking and entertaining but often wound up missing the party because of the over ambitious menus I planned.
I'd picture my guests and myself at the table, deep in conversation, or gathered around the stove, laughing and enjoying each other's company, but it's kind of hard to connect with people when you're desperately trying to spin threads of caramel on a humid summer day, or attempting to make cantaloupe mousse in January when the melons are hard as a rock. Yes, I did that. I was a harried hostess because I totally misunderstood the meaning of hospitality.
Then I met Shelby.
When I first met her I was a mess, depressed and depleted from a seemingly endless season of family struggles, illness, job loss and the resulting financial stress. Shelby heard about it and invited me to her lakeside home for what she called a "little retreat." When I pulled into her driveway, I saw a small-scale Airstream trailer parked near the entrance. Shelby greeted me, handed me the key to the trailer and told me to stay as long as I liked. I could have stayed forever. Shelby had papered the ceiling and walls with maps, murals and posters of

exotic vacation spots; reading materials were stacked next to a comfy built-in bed, soothing music played in the background and there was a note encouraging me to walk down to the lake or take a nap if I wanted. A few glorious hours later, she knocked on the door carrying a tray with tea and coffee and cookies. By the time I went home, I felt like a new woman — I will never forget her or that afternoon.

Someone who I didn't even know had seen a need and realized they had the means to address it. In the book *Radical Hospitality*, it says, 'Hospitality is the overflowing of a heart that has to share what it has received.' Shelby showed me hospitality by first, perceiving the need, and second, by sharing what she'd received: the gift of creativity. She employed her gift to create a place of respite for the weary and the hurting."

QUESTION for discussion with others: What gifts or talents have you been given that you could share with others? Freely giving them away ensures that your own Divine Supply will never run out.
— by Susan Ely
http://thesharedtable.com

2. Albert Einstein once said: "The most important question a person can ask is, "Is the Universe a friendly place?" Discuss your answer(s) to this question with others. On a scale of 1 to 100, how friendly would you say the Universe is? What would make it friendlier?

B. Journaling Themes

- "Practicing hospitality involves a certain recklessness."
- "Hospitality challenges us to work through our attitudes toward property and possessions."
- "A life of hospitality means a more continual interaction with others, and fewer opportunities to carefully project a "perfect image."
- "Even the crudest hospitality can work miracles."

(quotes from *Making Room* by Christine Pohl)

C. Hospitality in Film

Watch one of the films listed below and then journal about and/ or discuss with your group regarding the spiritual practice of hospitality as represented in the film.

1. Babette's Feast (1987)

Chefs are artists, this Oscar-winning drama reminds us, and like any other creators, their art has the power to change people's lives.

2. Chocolat (2000)

Juliette Binoche brings her lovely emotional translucence to Vianne Rocher, a free-spirited drifter who travels from town to town and opens a chocolaterie everywhere she lives.

Discussion questions for both films:

a. The preparation and eating of food is a large part of the film. What is the significance of this, and what do the attitudes of the main characters towards food show about their personalities?
b. Do you see yourself in the film?
c. What moved you the most in the film?
d. What lessons from the film would you like to incorporate into your daily life?

e. How important is following the rules?
f. What does this film have to say about hospitality?

D. "Hospitality" Collage
Create a collage out of paper, pictures from magazines etc., natural items….that helps you to visually explore what it means to practice hospitality. Use one of the quotes from section B: Journaling Themes, above if you need a focus. Share your collage with others on the retreat with you after you have finished.

Gather supplies: magazines, found objects, photos, drawings etc. cardboard, wood or other sturdy object to glue the collage pieces onto, glue stick or rubber cement,

Create collage: by positioning cut out or torn pieces of paper onto the cardboard backing to make a unified design. You may want to put a few pieces in place and play with their position before permanently affixing them.

Finishing: after your collage is complete, spray with a shellac to seal or use Mod-Podge sealer. Brush a thin layer of the Mod-Podge over the entire collage using a foam craft brush and then let dry. The Mod-Podge dries clear.

Silence
Spend some time (15-20 minutes minimum) sitting or walking in silence as a way to process the activities and messages of the day.

Closing Ritual — see pages 175-177 for activity choices

Closing Readings — see pages 178-185 for reading choices

Departure

RETREAT THREE - CONNECTION
We may think we're alone and many times may feel alone but we are all connected....the people, the animals, the plants, the systems.... Being separate is an illusion. Everything is interrelated, interconnected. The spiritual practice of connection is about acknowledging and recognizing your connectedness with all of life.
Stephen Mitchell says that the point of all spiritual practice is to wake up from the dream of the separate self. What things do I do in my daily life to perpetuate that dream of the separate self? How will I need to change in order to engage in the spiritual practice of connection?

Arrival
If you are retreating alone - use this time to unencumber: turn off phones, acquaint yourself with the space and set

up the space the way you will want it for the day, unpack supplies.

If you are retreating in a group, use this time to unencumber as described above PLUS:
Give everyone the opportunity to introduce themselves if appropriate, tell a little about their life at present, and also tell what items they are putting away for the day so they will be able to be as present as possible during the retreat.

Candle Lighting and Readings
Light a candle and choose several passages to read aloud from the following list as a way to center everyone's attention on the retreat theme.

a. The important element is the way in which all things are connected. Every thought and action sends shivers of energy into the world around us, which affects all creation. Perceiving the world as a web of connectedness helps us to

overcome the feelings of separation that hold us back and cloud our vision. This connection with all life increases our sense of responsibility for every move, every attitude, allowing us to see clearly that each soul does indeed make a difference to the whole.
— Emma Restall Orr

b. A wider, more altruistic attitude is very relevant in today's world. If we look at the situation from various angles, such as the complexity and interconnectedness of the nature of modern existence, then we will gradually notice a change in our outlook, so that when we say 'others' and when we think of others, we will no longer dismiss them as something that is irrelevant to us. We will no longer feel indifferent.
— The Dalai Lama

c. Strange is our situation here upon earth. Each of us comes for a short visit, not knowing why, yet sometimes seeming to a divine purpose. From the standpoint of daily life, however, there is one thing we do know: That we are here for the sake of others...for the countless unknown souls with whose fate we are connected by a bond of sympathy. Many

times a day, I realize how much my outer and inner life is built upon the labors of people, both living and dead, and how earnestly I must exert myself in order to give in return as much as I have received.
— Albert Einstein

d. Man did not weave the web of life, he is merely a strand in it. Whatever he does to the web, he does to himself.
— Chief Seattle

e. When the body sinks into death, the essence of man is revealed. Man is a knot, a web, a mesh into which relationships are tied. Only those relationships matter. The body is an old crock that nobody will miss. I have never known a man to think of himself when dying. Never.
— Antoine de Saint-Exupery

f. We will only bear pain to the degree that we feel connected.
— Kent Hoffman

g. Interdependence is and ought to be as much the ideal of man as self-sufficiency. Man is a social being. Without interrelation with society he cannot realize his oneness with the universe or suppress his egotism. His social interdependence enables him to test his faith and to prove himself on the touchstone of reality.
— Mahatma Gandhi

Listening
Allow some time, 30 minutes or more, for each person to go off on their own and process the opening readings. The readings can be written on a large piece of paper for participants to refer to or they can be printed on slips of paper for each person. This time allows for the processing of the words within the hearts and minds of each individual. Participants may want to sit/walk with the readings and then journal about their relationship to the readings and any other insights they notice during this time, or they may want to use their journals as a place in which to have a

conversation with themselves and/or the Divine on the topic.

Reflection
"Hearts need education and refinement just as the body needs exercise and moderation." Kabir Helminski, a Sufi sheikh

The activities in this section are intended to give retreat participants the opportunity to have a relationship with the retreat theme…to reflect, to re-create, co-create themselves in the light of their experiences. This can be done in many ways but the ultimate goal is to open oneself to the theme and find ways to incorporate the messages from the listening session into one's being. Participants may want to choose just one activity and spend the allotted time on that one pursuit or they may want to choose a couple of things to spend their time on. Groups may choose to all do the same thing for a time and then come back together to discuss the activity.

A. Small Group Discussion Questions

1. "If we see humility as self-knowledge, that's a very attractive virtue for modern

people. Everyone wants to know themselves, and I think in coming to know yourself you need community, you need relationship, because you can't know yourself in isolation. You don't exist in isolation."

by Laurence Freeman, Trinity Institute Benedictine Spirituality

QUESTIONS: What specific parts of yourself do you understand better by being in relationship with others? How are your friends and relations mirrors for you?
2. How has "labeling" others limited our ability to see them authentically?
How could we get away from labeling? Do we really need the little boxes we put people into?

3. How has the temptation to retreat into individualism kept us from becoming fully human, fully alive? How can we create a community that honors vulnerability?

B. Journaling Themes

- Make a list of the experiences you have had that support your sense of connection.

- "How could drops of water know themselves to be a river? Yet the river flows on." (Antoine de Saint-Exupery)
What does this quote mean to you?

- What, other than death, is part of our shared and common humanity?

- "I have been living in Hawaii for a time, and there's a huge military presence there. Every armed service has at least one base on the island of Oahu alone. When troops were beginning to be deployed to the Persian Gulf, some women of our church who had been making Anglican prayer beads were asked to make some for the troops. They got, like, fifty volunteers. Whole families would come. They ended up making and distributing over 1200. Some of them were literally given to troops as they boarded the plane. They were given out by the military chaplains. With each set of beads was a little note from St. Clements's Church with information on how to pray the beads, but also saying one could simply touch them and remember someone back home is praying for you.

Well, this little project made the newspapers and of course we got a few calls from people accusing us of aiding and abetting murderers. But I found it interesting in a church that some of the same people who were marching on every peace march in town were also making beads. One man told me that in the process of stringing the beads and making the knots and thinking of the young men and women who would carry them made him meditate on what it means to be one in Christ. It's not necessarily comfortable and it's beyond what we're capable for ourselves, but it is a truth that Christ does make us one against all polarities."

(Kathleen Norris at theTrinity Institute Benedictine Spirituality Conference, 2003)

QUESTIONS: What is your response to this reading? What would you say to the people who say that the church is aiding and abetting murderers? What would you say to Kathleen Norris about her assertion that being part of the body of Christ, or humanity in general, makes us one against all polarities?

- When do you feel most spiritually connected and how can you strengthen that connection?

C. Indra's Net
Create a visual representation of *Indra's Net* as a drawing, painting, weaving, found object sculpture, collage, or other art form. OR write a short story or poem using the ideas from Indra's Net.

Indra's Net:
Far away in the magnificent heavens where the great god Indra resides, there is a glistening net which has been hung so that it stretches out infinitely in all directions. In an extravagant gesture of love, the Indra has hung a single glittering jewel in each section of the net where the strands cross. The net itself has infinite dimensions so the jewels are

infinite in number. The jewels hang like glittering stars of the highest glory. It is a wonder to behold. If we could select one of these jewels to look at closely, we would discover that in its shining surface there are reflected *all* the other jewels in the net — an infinite in number. Not only that, but each of the jewels reflected in this one jewel is also reflecting all the other jewels, so that the picture of the reflection is infinite.

D. "Connection" Collage
Create a collage out of paper, pictures from magazines etc., natural items….that helps you to visually explore what it means to practice connection. Use one of the quotes from section B: Journaling Themes, above if you need a focus. Share your collage with others on the retreat with you after you have finished.
<u>Gather supplies:</u> magazines, found objects, photos, drawings etc. cardboard, wood or other sturdy object to glue the collage pieces onto, glue stick or rubber cement,
<u>Create collage:</u> by positioning cut out or torn pieces of paper onto the cardboard backing to make a unified design. You

may want to put a few pieces in place and play with their position before permanently affixing them.

Finishing: after your collage is complete, spray with a shellac to seal or use Mod-Podge sealer. Brush a thin layer of the Mod-Podge over the entire collage using a foam craft brush and then let dry. The Mod-Podge dries clear.

Silence
Spend some time (15-20 minutes minimum) sitting or walking in silence as a way to process the activities and messages of the day.

Closing Ritual — see pages 175-177 for activity choices

Closing Readings — see pages 178-185 for reading choices

Departure

RETREAT FOUR - IMAGINATION
Living a life with an engaged imagination means to not only dwell in possibilities but to keep one's mind and spirit open to the creative energy that flows through the universe. It not only means creating symbols and stories, it also means listening to ourselves and being willing to envision another way of doing things. It may mean that what one sees as "real" differs from what others see. What does a spiritual practice where imagination is cultivated look like? What is the difference between what is imagined and what is "real?"

_____

Arrival
If you are retreating alone - use this time to unencumber: turn off phones, acquaint yourself with the space and set up the space the way you will want it for the day, unpack supplies.

If you are retreating in a group, use this time to unencumber as described above PLUS:
Give everyone the opportunity to introduce themselves if appropriate, tell a little about their life at present, and also tell what items they are putting away for the day so they will be able to be as present as possible during the retreat.

___

Candle Lighting and Readings
Light a candle and choose several passages to read aloud from the following list as a way to center everyone's attention on the retreat theme.

a. We tend to consider imagination too lightly, forgetting that the life we make, for ourselves individually and for the world as a whole, is shaped and limited only by the perimeters of our imagination. Things are as we imagine them to be, as we imagine them into existence.
— Thomas Moore

b.   There are no rules of architecture for a castle in the clouds.
— Gilbert K. Chesterton

c.   You have to imagine it possible before you can see something. You can have the evidence right in front of you, but if you can't imagine something that has never existed before, it's impossible.
— Rita Dove

d.   Imagination is more important than knowledge. For knowledge is limited to all we now know and understand, while imagination embraces the entire world, and all there ever will be to know and understand.
— Albert Einstein

e.   I believe that imagination is stronger than knowledge - myth is more potent than history - dreams are more powerful than facts - hope always triumphs over experience - laughter is the cure for grief - love is stronger than death
— Robert Fulghum

f. Every human has four endowments: self- awareness, conscience, independent will and creative imagination. These give us the ultimate human freedom….the power to choose, to respond, to change.
— Stephen R. Covey

Listening
Allow some time, 30 minutes or more, for each person to go off on their own and process the opening readings. The readings can be written on a large piece of paper for participants to refer to or they can be printed on slips of paper for each person. This time allows for the processing of the words within the hearts and minds of each individual. Participants may want to sit/walk with the readings and then journal about their relationship to the readings and any other insights they notice during this time, or they may want to use their journals as a place in which to have a conversation with themselves and/or the Divine on the topic.

Reflection

"Hearts need education and refinement just as the body needs exercise and moderation." Kabir Helminski, a Sufi sheikh

The activities in this section are intended to give retreat participants the opportunity to have a relationship with the retreat theme...to reflect, to re-create, co-create themselves in the light of their experiences. This can be done in many ways but the ultimate goal is to open oneself to the theme and find ways to incorporate the messages from the listening session into one's being. Participants may want to choose just one activity and spend the allotted time on that one pursuit or they may want to choose a couple of things to spend their time on. Groups may choose to all do the same thing for a time and then come back together to discuss the activity.

A. Small Group Discussion Questions

- "You may be mistaking 'imagination' for 'imaginary.' Imaginary points to something that doesn't exist; imagination points to our capacity to envision what might be brought into existence."
— Rabbi Rami Shapiro

- Have a discussion about the difference between the two. Give some examples of both. Where are the lines between the two?

- Rabbi Rami Shapiro says, "One way to use imagination is when reading sacred texts. Imagine all the different meanings a text has to offer, play with the words and the plot to see how many facets of truth a single text can reveal. Reread a favorite passage of Scripture and learn to engage the text imaginatively by inviting as many meanings to arise from it as you can." Choose a sacred story to play with in your group. If you can't think of one, two are copied below for you to use.

THE SPIDER AND THE CAVE
- A MUSLIM STORY

Muhammad awoke with a start, pulled his cloak tightly round him for warmth, and listened. He knew he had many enemies. When Muhammad began preaching in Mecca, telling people to get rid of the idols they worshipped and worship the one true Allah instead, many people had been angry. They had worshipped their idols for a long time and old habits die hard.

Muhammad said a quick prayer and then he woke his young student, Ali. "It is time," said the Prophet. There were people plotting to kill Muhammad, but he did not know when they would strike. Muhammad and his followers planned to leave Mecca for Medina very soon. The people in Medina wanted Muhammad as their leader. Muhammad had not been welcomed as warmly by the people in Mecca. Muhammad and his good friend, Abu Bakr, were planning to leave Mecca secretly in the middle of the night. Ali would put on Muhammad's coat and pretend to be asleep in the Prophet's bed. The trick would help Muhammad and Abu Bakr get to Medina safely.

As Ali put on his teacher's coat and lay down on his sleeping mat, he was nervous. His ears were intently trying to discern any footsteps that might be near so he could pretend to be asleep when the time came. A while after the Muhammad left for Medina, Ali heard voices: "Muhammad is asleep in his hut. We will wait for dawn to attack him lest he accuse us of using the darkness to our advantage."

When daylight came, the group of men plotting to kill Muhammad quietly surrounded the house where Ali was sleeping. They flung open the door, swords drawn, only to find Ali asleep on his mat. Ali was a young follower and of no consequence to them and the men yelled with disappointment and frustration.

Meanwhile Muhammad and Abu Bakr had been taking the back roads from Mecca to Medina so they would not be caught. They were forced to climb the rocky slopes near Mecca where there were many caves. They were dusty, tired, and thirsty. Abu Bakr was also afraid and angry because of his fear. He could not believe that the Prophet of God would be treated like this and he called to God for help. Muhammad kept assuring his friend that God would take care of them. By the time night had surrounded them they could hear the hooves of their enemies' horses and knew they were nearby searching for them. Abu Bakr began to cry out. "What shall we do? There are many of them and only two of us." Muhammad guided his friend into the nearest cave. "That is not so," he said. "There are three of us."

They heard footsteps at the entrance to the cave and Abu Bakr held his breath. As he held his breath he heard one of the enemies say, "No, they can't be in here. The entrance is covered with spider's webs and a lot of debris. It looks like no one has been here since Muhammad was born." Then there was the sound of horse's hooves leaving the area. Abu Bakr laughed and said a prayer of thanksgiving to God, but he did not move. What had they been talking about...spider's webs and branches?

He went to the opening of the cave and looked out. Over the entrance there was a beautiful, silver spider's web, and near it a large nest where a dove sat. Abu Bakr wondered aloud how all of those things had come to be at the cave entrance but the prophet simply smiled.

Soon the two friends left the cave and continued on toward Medina, safe and secure.

THE FEEDING OF THE MULITUDE - A CHRISTIAN STORY

Jesus had sent his disciples out into the country with the power to heal sick people and tell about God's love. When the disciples returned, they were very excited to tell Jesus what had happened on their journey but they had a hard time finding a place to be with him alone since the people who wanted to see Jesus followed the disciples everywhere they went hoping to get a glimpse of Jesus or to hear him teach.

Jesus knew the disciples wanted to talk to him so he suggested they get in a boat and go to a quiet place. But many people saw them leaving and recognized them and ran after them, following the boat along the shore. The windy day slowed the boat down so that the people reached the other shore where Jesus was headed before Jesus did and when he arrived a large crowd was waiting for him.

Jesus knew the people only wanted to see him because they needed someone to teach them and believe in them and he had great compassion for them. He thought the disciples would understand so he began talking to the large crowd instead of focusing only on the disciples.

As the day grew later and the people began to get hungry, Jesus suggested that the disciples get something to eat for everyone. The disciples answered: "There is no food around here. We should send the people away so they can go and get their own food."
Jesus replied, "You give them something to eat."

The disciples were shocked at Jesus' words and some thought that he had misunderstood them. It would take much more money than they had to feed this large crowd- Jesus should know that!

While the disciples were arguing among themselves, one of the disciples noticed a small boy walking up to Jesus with a small lunch. Jesus asked him what he had for his lunch and he talked to the boy for a moment. Jesus said to the disciples, "Here is a boy with five small loaves of bread and two small fish. How far do you think it will go among so many people?" The disciples continued to grumble to themselves.
Then Jesus smiled and said, "Ask the crowd to sit down."
There was a big grassy side of a hill there so everyone sat down. It seemed like there were about 5000 people gathered there- maybe more. After everyone was seated Jesus took the loaves of bread and the fish and held them up for all to see. Then he thanked God for the bread and asked the disciples to take them and pass them around. Everyone was instructed to take as much as they wanted. He did the same with the fish.

As the people ate they laughed and talked to their neighbors, sharing the stories of their lives. After everyone was full, Jesus asked the disciples to gather all the food that was leftover. After they gathered all the baskets of food they were amazed at how much was left. There were twelve baskets of bread and fish still left- enough for another meal tomorrow.

B. Journaling Themes

- "A rock pile ceases to be a rock pile the moment a single man contemplates it, bearing within him the image of a cathedral."
— Antoine de Saint-Exupery

- What things in your life have been changed from the ordinary to the extraordinary by the use of your imagination?

- "Think left and think right and think low and think high. Oh, the thinks you can think up if only you try! ….I like nonsense, it wakes up the brain cells. Fantasy is a necessary ingredient in living… it's a way of looking at life through the wrong end of a telescope. Which is what I do, and that enables you to laugh at life's realities."
 — Dr. Seuss
What kind of nonsense can you create today?

- "Imagine for yourself a character, a model personality, whose example you determine to follow, in private as well as in public."
— Epictetus

- "Trust that little voice in your head that says 'Wouldn't it be interesting if...'; and then do it."
— Duane Michals

C. Writing the Story of You
From each of the six pairs of words in the section below, choose three words that best describe you:
- gregarious or cautious
- political or a-political
- organized or disorderly
- quiet or noisy
- practical or impractical
- cautious or a gambler

Now choose six things that most appeal to you from the following pairs:
- an open window or a screened window
- a flashlight or a candle
- a river or a calm pool of water
- a computer or a pencil and paper

- a tortoise or a hare
- a coffee mug or a crystal goblet
- a smooth beach or a rocky trail
- a stone path or a ladder
- a flower or a pine cone
- a key or a hammer

Now use the three descriptors from the first section and the six items from the second section to write a story about you.

C. "Imagination" Collage
Create a collage out of paper, pictures from magazines etc., natural items....that helps you to visually explore what it means to practice imagination. Use one of the quotes from section B: Journaling Themes, above if you need a focus. Share your collage with others on the retreat with you after you have finished.

<u>Gather supplies:</u> magazines, found objects, photos, drawings etc. cardboard, wood or other sturdy object to glue the collage pieces onto, glue stick or rubber cement,

<u>Create collage:</u> by positioning cut out or torn pieces of paper onto the cardboard backing to make a unified design. You may want to put a few pieces in place

and play with their position before permanently affixing them.

Finishing: after your collage is complete, spray with a shellac to seal or use Mod-Podge sealer. Brush a thin layer of the Mod-Podge over the entire collage using a foam craft brush and then let dry. The Mod-Podge dries clear.

Silence
Spend some time (15-20 minutes minimum) sitting or walking in silence as a way to process the activities and messages of the day.

Closing Ritual — see pages 175-177 for activity choices

Closing Readings — see pages 178-185 for reading choices

Departure

RETREAT FIVE - GRATITUDE

Gratitude as a spiritual practice enriches our lives by helping us to see more clearly the individual components of our lives and express thanksgiving for those things. Even when our days go badly and we are sick or tired or in despair, we can usually find one or two things, at least, to be grateful for. Gratitude helps us to count our blessings one by one…to take time to say "thank you." Meister Eckhart has been quoted as saying: "If the only prayer you ever say in your whole life is "thank you," that would suffice."

What am I most grateful for? What are some things in my life I take for granted and need to express thanksgiving for?

Arrival

If you are retreating alone - use this time to unencumber: turn off phones, acquaint yourself with the space and set up the space the way you will want it for the day, unpack supplies.

If you are retreating in a group, use this time to unencumber as described above PLUS:
Give everyone the opportunity to introduce themselves if appropriate, tell a little about their life at present, and also tell what items they are putting away for the day so they will be able to be as present as possible during the retreat.

_____

Candle Lighting and Readings
Light a candle and choose several passages to read aloud from the following list as a way to center everyone's attention on the retreat theme.

a. The unthankful heart... discovers no mercies; but let the thankful heart sweep through the day and, as the magnet finds the iron, so it will find, in every hour, some heavenly blessings!
— Henry Ward Beech

b. Gratitude is a quality similar to electricity: it must be produced and discharged and used up in order to exist at all.
— William Faulkner

c. As we express our gratitude, we must never forget that the highest appreciation is not to utter words, but to live by them.
— John Fitzgerald Kennedy

d.. After sleeping through a hundred million centuries we have finally opened our eyes on a sumptuous planet, sparkling with color, bountiful with life. Within decades we must close our eyes again. Isn't it a noble, an enlightened way of spending our brief time in the sun, to work at understanding the universe and how we have come to wake up in it? This is how I answer when I am asked—as I am surprisingly often—why I bother to get up in the mornings.
— Richard Dawkins

e. Nothing that is done for you is a matter of course. Everything originates in a will for the good, which is directed at you. Train yourself never to put off the word or action for the expression of gratitude.
— Albert Schweitzer

f. Life without thankfulness is devoid of love and passion. Hope without thankfulness is lacking in fine perception. Faith without thankfulness lacks strength and fortitude. Every virtue divorced from thankfulness is maimed and limps along the spiritual road.
— John Henry Jowett

g. Can you see the holiness in those things you take for granted— a paved road or a washing machine? If you concentrate on finding what is good in every situation, you will discover that your life will suddenly be filled with gratitude, a feeling that nurtures the soul.
— Rabbi Harold Kushner

Listening

Allow some time, 30 minutes or more, for each person to go off on their own and process the opening readings. The readings can be written on a large piece of paper for participants to refer to or they can be printed on slips of paper for each person. This time allows for the processing of the words within the hearts and minds of each individual. Participants may want to sit/walk with the readings and then journal about their relationship to the readings and any other insights they notice during this time, or they may want to use their journals as a place in which to have a conversation with themselves and/or the Divine on the topic.

Reflection

"Hearts need education and refinement just as the body needs exercise and moderation." Kabir Helminski, a Sufi sheikh

The activities in this section are intended to give retreat participants the opportunity to have a relationship with the retreat theme…to reflect, to re-create, co-create themselves in the light of their experiences. This can be done in many ways but the ultimate goal is to open oneself to the theme and find ways to incorporate the messages from the listening session into one's being. Participants may want to choose just one activity and spend the allotted time on that one pursuit or they may want to choose a couple of things to spend their time on. Groups may choose to all do the same thing for a time and then come back together to discuss the activity.

A. Small Group Discussion Questions & Activities

- Discuss the following quotes individually and as a pair:

1. "What if you gave someone a gift, and they neglected to thank you for it- would you be likely to give them another? Life is the same way. In order to attract more of the blessings that life has to offer, you must truly appreciate what you already have."
— Ralph Marsten

2. "But the value of gratitude does not consist solely in getting you more blessings in the future. Without gratitude you cannot long keep from dissatisfied thought regarding things as they are."
— Wallace Wattles

Talk for a few minutes, as a group, about gratitude and its importance in your life.

Next, each person takes a piece of paper and a pen and writes down all of the things they can think of to be grateful for.

After the lists are made, each person goes out for a walk and collects one small pebble (about the size of a marble) for each item on their list and puts each one in their pocket(s).

As more items are added to the lists, more rocks are added to the pockets. Keep the rocks in your pockets until the end of the retreat.

Find a time to process this exercise before the closing ritual of the retreat.

QUESTIONS: What difference did it make to be able to physically feel the weight of the gratitude lists?

Would it make a difference to your attitude if you could feel that weight each day?

B. Journaling Themes

- "You simply will not be the same person two months from now after consciously giving thanks each day for the abundance that exists in your life. And you will have set in motion an ancient spiritual law: The more you have and are grateful for, the more will be given you."
— Sarah Ban Breathnach
Do you agree?

- List all of the ways you express gratitude in your life.
- Can a person truly express gratitude if they do not believe in God, a Higher Power or something up there watching out for you?

C. Gratitude Postcards
Create postcards on 3x5 or larger notecards and send them to people in your life you are especially grateful for. Try to think of people or organizations

you might not ordinarily thank and might even take for granted like mail carriers, gym receptionists or a local business. You can create the cards by writing quotes, gluing interesting pictures cut out of magazines or printed off the internet, or by drawing cartoons expressing your gratitude. Mail the cards as soon as you get home. If cards are not a standard postcard size and weight put them in a stamped envelope to mail.

D. Memorize a Prayer of Gratitude

- Let your eyes look deep within
Find the blessings you've been given
Feel your heart overflow in gratitude
Then lift your soul right up to heaven.
— Renée Miller

- When the heart is grateful, pushed outward in praise
Even troubles hard to bear, heavenward are raised.
Let God's blessing come to you, let your soul be still
Then release the blessings to the world at will.
— Renée Miller

> - I thank You God for
> most this amazing
> day: for the leaping
> greenly spirits of trees
> and a blue true dream
> of sky; and for
> everything
> which is natural which
> is infinite which is yes
> — e. e. Cumming

This Creative Day — When Giving Thanks by William Cleary

Strong, evolutionary God,
we bless you for this creative day,
for all the novelty and variation
that surrounds each moment
with possibility and hope.

We bless you for the life we have.
We bless you for energy and intelligence,
especially the energies of love and inventiveness.
We bless you for the future.
for each self-reproducing molecule in our bodies
that sweetly carries from one generation

to the next
the instructions for design of future living things
linked to us
and encompassed in our love.
We desire today to be instruments
of your open-ended dreams.
May it be so.

E. "Gratitude" Collage
Create a collage out of paper, pictures from magazines etc., natural items….that helps you to visually explore what it means to practice gratitude. Use one of the quotes from section B: Journaling Themes, above if you need a focus. Share your collage with others on the retreat with you after you have finished.
<u>Gather supplies:</u> magazines, found objects, photos, drawings etc. cardboard, wood or other sturdy object to glue the collage pieces onto, glue stick or rubber cement,
<u>Create collage:</u> by positioning cut out or torn pieces of paper onto the cardboard backing to make a unified design. You may want to put a few pieces in place and play with their position before permanently affixing them.

Finishing: after your collage is complete, spray with a shellac to seal or use Mod-Podge sealer. Brush a thin layer of the Mod-Podge over the entire collage using a foam craft brush and then let dry. The Mod-Podge dries clear.

Silence
Spend some time (15-20 minutes minimum) sitting or walking in silence as a way to process the activities and messages of the day.

Closing Ritual — see pages 175-177 for activity choices

Closing Readings — see pages 178-185 for reading choices

Departure

RETREAT SIX - SILENCE

The spiritual practice of silence is not just about making time in a busy schedule to experience silence. It is also about valuing silence as a part of life instead of filling the day up with noise and activity. In this time in the history of our world, it is almost certain that you will not experience silence unless you intentionally build it in to your life. Yet, even when our surroundings are silent, quieting the mind is another thing altogether. This spiritual practice is especially challenging because of the inner and outer work involved. Where can I build time into my days to experience silence? What might I have to sacrifice to do so?

Arrival

If you are retreating alone - use this time to unencumber: turn off phones, acquaint yourself with the space and set up the space the way you will want it for the day, unpack supplies.

If you are retreating in a group, use this time to unencumber as described above PLUS:
Give everyone the opportunity to introduce themselves if appropriate, tell a little about their life at present, and also tell what items they are putting away for the day so they will be able to be as present as possible during the retreat.

Candle Lighting and Readings
Light a candle and choose several passages to read aloud from the following list as a way to center everyone's attention on the retreat theme.

a. Effective Silence
God of wisdom,
teach me to relate to others
with words they need to hear,
with words
that will never misguide.
Teach me, dear God,
that often the most effective words
are no words at all.

Teach me how to communicate
with that most potent gift
of silence.
— Rebbe Nachman of Breslov

b. In the attitude of silence the soul finds the path in a clearer light, and what is elusive and deceptive resolves itself into crystal clearness. Our life is a long and arduous quest after Truth.
— Mahatma Gandhi

c. There is no need to go to India or anywhere else to find peace. You will find that deep place of silence right in your room, your garden or even your bathtub.
— Elisabeth Kübler-Ross

d. Silence is like a river of grace inviting us to leap unafraid into its beckoning depths. It is dark and mysterious in the waters of grace. Yet in the silent darkness we are given new eyes. In the heart of the divine we can see more clearly who we are. We are renewed and cleansed in this river of

silence. There are those among you who fear the Great Silence. It is a foreign land to you. Sometimes it is good to leap into the unknown. Practice leaping.
— Macrina Wiederkehr

e. When you become aware of silence, immediately there is that state of inner still alertness. You are present. You have stepped out of thousands of years of collective human conditioning.
— Eckhart Tolle

f. Soon silence will have passed into legend. Man has turned his back on silence. Day after day he invents machines and devices that increase noise and distract humanity from the essence of life, contemplation, meditation... tooting, howling, screeching, booming, crashing, whistling, grinding, and trilling bolster his ego. His anxiety subsides. His inhuman void spreads monstrously like a gray vegetation.
 — Jean Arp

g. Not merely an absence of noise, Real Silence begins when a reasonable being withdraws from the noise in order to find peace and order in his inner sanctuary.
— Peter Minard

Listening
Allow some time, 30 minutes or more, for each person to go off on their own and process the opening readings. The readings can be written on a large piece of paper for participants to refer to or they can be printed on slips of paper for each person. This time allows for the processing of the words within the hearts and minds of each individual. Participants may want to sit/walk with the readings and then journal about their relationship to the readings and any other insights they notice during this time, or they may want to use their journals as a place in which to have a conversation with themselves and/or the Divine on the topic.

Reflection
"Hearts need education and refinement just as the body needs exercise and moderation." Kabir Helminski, a Sufi sheikh

The activities in this section are intended to give retreat participants the opportunity to have a relationship with the retreat theme...to reflect, to re-create, co-create themselves in the light of their experiences. This can be done in many ways but the ultimate goal is to open oneself to the theme and find ways to incorporate the messages from the listening session into one's being. Participants may want to choose just one activity and spend the allotted time on that one pursuit or they may want to choose a couple of things to spend their time on. Groups may choose to all do the same thing for a time and then come back together to discuss the activity.

A. Walking Meditation
In case it isn't obvious, this kind of meditation is done with the eyes open. Choose a place to walk that is away

from traffic and on a level surface so that you can walk without paying too much attention to obstacles. You might begin with a 20-minute walk, although it is up to you how long you walk. It all depends on how much time you have. The purpose of this kind of meditation is to develop a greater awareness and a greater understanding of yourself. It is also a practice that lends itself well to silence and can be done on a short walk through a parking lot or on a wooded trail during a lunch break.

As you begin, simply stand in place and feel your feet on the earth. Feel the way your feet balance your body on the ground. As you begin to walk, walk at a slow but normal pace. Be aware of your foot as the heel makes contact with the ground first and then as your foot rolls forward onto the ball, and then as it lifts and travels through the air. Be aware of how your foot feels in your shoe, of your ankles and how relaxed they are, of your calves and knees and thighs as you walk.

Follow your awareness up your body to your neck and then, eventually, to the top of your head, relaxing all of those parts as you continue to walk. Notice your jaw especially… is it relaxed? If not, try to relax it.

Are you bored or content or agitated? Are you feeling happy or sad? Notice your emotions. Is your mind busy, or is it calm? Are you thinking about things unconnected with this practice? For now, just notice these things and then let them go, with no particular judgment.

Slowly but purposefully, breathe in and out as you walk in silence.
Continue your walk for as long as you have allotted for this practice. You may want to journal about this experience or discuss it with others who are on retreat with you at the end of the day.

B. Journaling Themes

- *Noise* by Anthony De Mello, *One Minute Wisdom*
"Each day the master would be inundated with questions that he would reply to seriously, playfully, gently, firmly.
One disciple always sat through each session in silence.

When someone questioned her about it, she said,
"I hardly hear a word he says. I am too distracted by his silence."

- The art of being a monk is to know how to be in the desert (withdrawal from people and activity to meet God) and how to be in the market-place (involvement with people in one way or another). That is why in our monastic life we provide, in terms of time and place, a desert- that is, a desert situation- where silence is precious, silence required. We are foolish when we think in terms of rules of silence, as if these were an external discipline imposed because monastic life should have discipline. Rather, we should see these places and times of silence as the very basis of a mature, adult spiritual life. We should not see silence as an interruption of our recreation; we should see our recreation as punctuating our silence…..We can, too, escape to the market-place because we fear the desert, because we are fearful of solitude, fearful of silence…..We shall never be safe in the market-place unless we are at home in the desert…..The heart, too, must learn to live in its desert if it is to be capable of

involvement in the market-place. It is only in the desert that you can learn to turn loneliness into solitude, and it is only when we have learned solitude and freedom- the capacity to be alone- that we can safely be involved with others.
— Cardinal Basil Hume, O.S.B.,
 in *The Intentional Life: The Making of a Spiritual Vocation*

- When I was teaching I had a handmade poster in a frame on a shelf that read, "Don't just do something, sit there." Those words weren't my own, but I liked the concept because the message signaled a shift in my productivity-centered paradigm toward an understanding of the value of balancing doing and non-doing………I worked at a public elementary school in which some members of the faculty did not want benches, picnic tables, or other seating on the playground for the children for fear they would just sit and do nothing. Can we come to see that simply being still is beneficial in itself? How are the first flowers of spring discovered, the fluid shapes of clouds observed, or the

fragrance of dried autumn leaves taken in, if we are in constant motion?
— Cathleen Haskins

QUESTIONS: Have you ever been given permission to NOT do something, just sit there?   Can you remember times in your life when you have "just sat and done nothing?" What did you discover about yourself and your world?

<u>- A Parable from the Sufi tradition:</u>
Three monks who had taken vows of silence were permitted an annual reprieve during which one monk was permitted to speak at the end of each year of silence.

At the end of the first year, the first monk was allowed his opportunity to speak, whereupon he said: *The soup is too hot.*

Another year elapsed. Then it was the next monk's turn. The monks turned their attention to him, whereupon he said: *The soup is too cold.*

Another year elapsed. It was the third monk's turn. The assembled monks turned to him, whereupon he said: *The soup is neither too cold nor too hot. However, it is too salty.*

By the fourth year, the Abbess had posted a notice that it would be she who would speak at the end of that year. The assembled monks were particularly alert to hear the esteemed Abbess give her speech. One could
hear the sound of a butterfly's wings in the silence which enveloped the hall. Whereupon the Abbess said: *There will be no more of this quibbling about the soup. Thus have I heard.*

- Father Thomas Merton said in solitude he discovered that it was not words that interrupted his silence, it was the urge to speak.

C. Silence in Film
Watch the film, *Into Great Silence (2005),* and then journal about and/ or discuss with your group regarding the spiritual practice of silence as represented in the film.

In this contemplative documentary from filmmaker Philip Gröning, the Grande Chartreuse monastery opens its doors to the public for the first time since being founded by St. Bruno in 1084 to offer an intimate look at a lifestyle rarely experienced by those outside of the brotherhood.

Discussion questions for the film:

a. Do you see yourself in the film?
b. What in the film moved you the most?
c. What lessons from the film would you like to incorporate into your daily life?
d. How important is following the rules?
e. What does this film have to say about silence and devotion to silence as a way of life?
f. Of what value to society is this way of living?

D. "Silence" Collage
Create a collage out of paper, pictures from magazines etc., natural items….that helps you to visually explore what it means to practice silence. Use one of the quotes from section B: Journaling Themes, above if you need a focus. Share your collage

with others on the retreat with you after you have finished.

Gather supplies: magazines, found objects, photos, drawings etc. cardboard, wood or other sturdy object to glue the collage pieces onto, glue stick or rubber cement,

Create collage: by positioning cut out or torn pieces of paper onto the cardboard backing to make a unified design. You may want to put a few pieces in place and play with their position before permanently affixing them.

Finishing: after your collage is complete, spray with a shellac to seal or use Mod-Podge sealer. Brush a thin layer of the Mod-Podge over the entire collage using a foam craft brush and then let dry. The Mod-Podge dries clear.

Silence

Spend some time (15-20 minutes minimum) sitting or walking in silence as a way to process the activities and messages of the day.

Closing Ritual — see pages 175-177 for activity choices

Closing Readings — see pages 178-185 for reading choices

Departure

RETREAT SEVEN - WONDER

A sense of wonder is fed by a curiosity about the universe. It helps us to broaden our views and be open to possibilities, to notice when we experience awe or amazement. The other side of wonder is asking questions- pondering the origins of the universe or the gifts of the earth. People who cultivate the spiritual practice of wonder use all of their resources: body, mind, and spirit, to engage life. Like its cousins openness and imagination, wonder calls us to listen and wait. Where do I find wonder in my daily life? Can one have enough wonder in one's life? How does one learn to value wonder and notice it more?

Arrival

If you are retreating alone - use this time to unencumber: turn off phones, acquaint yourself with the space and set up the space the way you will want it for the day, unpack supplies.

If you are retreating in a group, use this time to unencumber as described above PLUS:

Give everyone the opportunity to introduce themselves if appropriate, tell a little about their life at present, and also tell what items they are putting away for the day so they will be able to be as present as possible during the retreat.

Candle Lighting and Readings

Light a candle and choose several passages to read aloud from the following list as a way to center everyone's attention on the retreat theme.

a. The most beautiful thing we can experience is the mysterious. It is the source of all true art and all science. He to whom this emotion is a stranger, who can no longer pause to wonder and stand rapt in awe, is as good as dead: his eyes are closed.
— Albert Einstein

b. Whether one sees the world as God's creation or as a secular mystery that science is on the way to figuring out, there is no denying the beauty and majesty of everything from mountain ranges, deserts, and rain forests to the exquisite details in the design of an ordinary mosquito.
— Robert C. Solomon

c. People travel to wonder at the height of the mountains, at the huge waves of the seas, at the long course of the rivers, at the vast compass of the ocean, at the circular motion of the stars, and yet they pass by themselves without wondering.
— Augustine

d. We are so impressed by scientific clank that we feel we ought not to say that the sunflower turns because it knows where the sun is. It is almost second nature to us to prefer explanations . . . with a large vocabulary. We are much more comfortable when we are assured that the sunflower turns because it is heliotropic. The trouble with that kind of talk is that it tempts us to think that we

know what the sunflower is up to. But we don't. The sunflower is a mystery, just as every single thing in the universe is.
— Robert Farrer Capon

e. Two things fill me with constantly increasing admiration and awe, the longer and more earnestly I reflect on them: the starry heavens without and the moral law within.
— Immanuel Kant

f. People usually consider walking on water or in thin air a miracle. But I think the real miracle is not to walk either on water or in thin air, but to walk on earth. Every day we are engaged in a miracle which we don't even recognize: a blue sky, white clouds, green leaves, the black, curious eyes of a child — our own two eyes. All is a miracle.
— Thich Nhat Hanh

g. The possession of knowledge does not kill the sense of wonder and mystery. There is always more mystery.
— Anaïs Nin

Listening
Allow some time, 30 minutes or more, for each person to go off on their own and process the opening readings. The readings can be written on a large piece of paper for participants to refer to or they can be printed on slips of paper for each person. This time allows for the processing of the words within the hearts and minds of each individual. Participants may want to sit/walk with the readings and then journal about their relationship to the readings and any other insights they notice during this time, or they may want to use their journals as a place in which to have a conversation with themselves and/or the Divine on the topic.

Reflection
"Hearts need education and refinement just as the body needs exercise and moderation." Kabir Helminski, a Sufi sheikh

The activities in this section are intended to give retreat participants the opportunity to have a relationship with the retreat theme…to reflect, to re-

create, co-create themselves in the light of their experiences. This can be done in many ways but the ultimate goal is to open oneself to the theme and find ways to incorporate the messages from the listening session into one's being. Participants may want to choose just one activity and spend the allotted time on that one pursuit or they may want to choose a couple of things to spend their time on. Groups may choose to all do the same thing for a time and then come back together to discuss the activity.

A. Small Group Discussion Questions & Activities

- "I dreamed I was a butterfly, flitting around in the sky; then I awoke. Now I wonder: Am I a man who dreamt of being a butterfly, or am I a butterfly dreaming that I am a man?"
— Chuang Tzu

- Go for a walk as a group and notice the wonders of nature that surround you. Wonder aloud. Ask questions about the how and why of what you see. Maybe someone in your group knows the answer to your question. Maybe no one does. Let it be okay to ask questions that have no immediate answers.

- Imagine you are 100 years old, sitting in a rocking chair on your porch; you can feel the autumn breeze gently brushing against your face. You are happy, and pleased with the life you have lived. Look back at your life and all that you've achieved, acquired, and all the relationships you've cultivated. What matters to you most now?

B. Journaling Themes

- Make a list of the awesome or amazing things you have encountered in your life. What lessons did you learn from your experiences?

- If happiness was the national currency, what kind of work would make you rich?

- If you could offer a newborn child only one piece of advice, what would it be?

- Why are you, you?

C. Koans to Ponder
- *A Cup of Tea*
A Japanese master was visiting with a university professor who came to inquire about Zen. They were seated in the master's study and the master served tea. He poured his visitor's cup full, and then kept on pouring. The professor watched the overflow until he no longer could restrain himself.
"It is overfull. No more will go in!"
"Like this cup," the master said, "you are full of your own opinions and speculations. How can I teach you unless you first empty your cup?"

- *Two Souls*
Nonin had a very beautiful daughter named See. He also had a handsome young cousin named Pavel. As they grew, Nonin often commented that they would make a fine match as a married couple but in reality he planned to pledge his daughter in marriage to someone other than Pavel. Having heard Nonin's suggestion that they would make a good couple all of their lives, See and Pavel took Nonin's suggestion seriously. They fell in love and considered themselves engaged. One day Nonin announced that See was

to marry a man other than Pavel. In rage and despair, Pavel left by boat. After he had been at sea for several days, he was overjoyed to discover that See was in the boat with him.

The couple went to a coastal city where they lived for many years and had two children. But, even though they had a happy life, See could not forget her father; so the couple decided to go back and ask for Nonin's forgiveness and blessing. When they arrived, See remained on the boat. Pavel went to his cousin's house, humbly apologized for taking See away and asked forgiveness for them both.

"What is the meaning of all of your mad talk?" Nonin exclaimed. He told Pavel that See had fallen ill immediately after Pavel had left many years ago and had been in a coma since that day. Pavel told Nonin that he was astonished by that news, that it could not be true and he would show him why not. Then Pavel went to the boat and brought See to her father's house. When See entered the house, the See lying ill in bed got up and went to meet the See from the boat and the two became one.

According to the legend, See had two souls, one always sick at home and the other a married woman with two children. Which was the true soul?

- The Best
One day a seeker was walking through a market. He overheard a woman say to the fruit vendor, "Give me the best melon you have." "You cannot find anything in my stand that is not the best." At these words, the seeker was enlightened.

D. What Do You Value?
Select your top 5 and list in order of importance and discuss your choices with others or journal about your choices.

Achievement - Adventure - Beauty
Challenge - Comfort   Courage
Creativity - Curiosity - Education
Empowerment - Excelling - Family
Financial Freedom - Fitness
Friendship - Giving/Service - Health
Honesty -   Independence
Inner Peace - Integrity - Intelligence
Intimacy - Joy - Leadership

Learning - Love - Motivation - Passion
Performance - Personal Growth
Play - Productivity - Reliability
Respect - Security - Spirituality
Success - Time - Work

E. "Wonder" Collage

Create a collage out of paper, pictures from magazines etc., natural items….that helps you to visually explore what it means to practice wonder. Use one of the quotes from section B: Journaling Themes, above if you need a focus. Share your collage with others on the retreat with you after you have finished.

<u>Gather supplies:</u> magazines, found objects, photos, drawings etc. cardboard, wood or other sturdy object to glue the collage pieces onto, glue stick or rubber cement,

<u>Create collage:</u> by positioning cut out or torn pieces of paper onto the cardboard backing to make a unified design. You may want to put a few pieces in place and play with their position before permanently affixing them.

<u>Finishing:</u> after your collage is complete, spray with a shellac to seal or use Mod-Podge sealer. Brush a thin layer of the

Mod-Podge over the entire collage using a foam craft brush and then let dry. The Mod-Podge dries clear.

Silence
Spend some time (15-20 minutes minimum) sitting or walking in silence as a way to process the activities and messages of the day.

Closing Ritual — see pages 175-177 for activity choices

Closing Readings — see pages 178-185 for reading choices

Departure

RETREAT EIGHT — PLAY

"Creative people are curious, flexible, persistent, and independent with a tremendous spirit of adventure and a love of play." — Henri Matisse

The spiritual practice of play may not be something you have ever considered before. In western culture we expect play from children but not adults. However, the ability to engage in healthy play during one's lifetime is important if one is to be engaged in life in a creative and adaptive way. George Bernard Shaw said, "We don't stop playing because we grow old; we grow old because we stop playing." Play helps us to keep a balanced perspective and opens our mind to new possibilities. How can I incorporate more play into my days? What "play" do I long to do that I have not had the courage to do or made the time to do?

Arrival

If you are retreating alone - use this time to unencumber: turn off phones, acquaint yourself with the space and set up the space the way you will want it for the day, unpack supplies.

If you are retreating in a group, use this time to unencumber as described above PLUS:
Give everyone the opportunity to introduce themselves if appropriate, tell a little about their life at present, and also tell what items they are putting away for the day so they will be able to be as present as possible during the retreat.

Candle Lighting and Readings
Light a candle and choose several passages to read aloud from the following list as a way to center everyone's attention on the retreat theme.

a. We are most nearly ourselves when we achieve the seriousness of a child at play.
— Heraclitus

b. You can discover more about a person in an hour of play than in a year of conversation.
— Plato

c. Almost all creativity involves purposeful play.
— Abraham Maslow

d. The very existence of youth is due in part to the necessity for play; the animal does not play because he is young, he has a period of youth because he must play.
— Karl Groos

e. If you want to be creative, stay in part a child, with the creativity and invention that characterizes children before they are deformed by adult society.
— Jean Piaget

f. It is in playing, and only in playing, that the individual child or adult is able to be creative and to use the whole personality, and it is only in being creative that the individual discovers the self.
— D.W. Winnicott

g. Ritual grew up in sacred play; poetry was born in play and nourished on play; music and dancing were pure play... We have to conclude, therefore, that civilization is, in its earliest phases, played. It does not come from play...it arises in and as play, and never leaves it.
— Johan Huizing

h. Pausing to listen to an airplane in the sky, stooping to watch a ladybug on a plant, sitting on a rock to watch the waves crash over the quayside—children have their own agendas and timescales. As they find out more about their world and their place in it; they work hard not to let adults hurry them. We need to hear their voices.
— Cathy Nutbrown

Listening
Allow some time, 30 minutes or more, for each person to go off on their own and process the opening readings. The readings can be written on a large piece of paper for participants to refer to or they can be printed on slips of paper for

each person. This time allows for the processing of the words within the hearts and minds of each individual. Participants may want to sit/walk with the readings and then journal about their relationship to the readings and any other insights they notice during this time, or they may want to use their journals as a place in which to have a conversation with themselves and/or the Divine on the topic.

Reflection

"Hearts need education and refinement just as the body needs exercise and moderation." Kabir Helminski, a Sufi sheikh

The activities in this section are intended to give retreat participants the opportunity to have a relationship with the retreat theme…to reflect, to re-create, co-create themselves in the light of their experiences. This can be done in many ways but the ultimate goal is to open oneself to the theme and find ways to incorporate the messages from the listening session into one's being. Participants may want to choose just one activity and spend the allotted time on that one pursuit or they may want to choose a couple of things to spend their time on. Groups may choose to all do the same thing for a time and then come back together to discuss the activity.

A. Small Group Discussion Questions & Activities

- "To the art of working well a civilized race would add the art of playing well."
— George Santayana

What does it mean to play well?

- "The opposite of play is not work. It's depression."
— Brian Sutton-Smith
Do you agree? Discuss the relationship between play and depression.

- Make play dough together as a group and then play together. This recipe makes approximately 2 cups. Plan for 1 cup per person.

Ingredients for play dough
2 cups flour
4 tablespoons cream of tartar
2 tablespoons cooking oil
1 cup salt
Food coloring
2 cups water

Instructions
Place all ingredients into a medium size saucepan.
Give mixture a stir.
Continue to stir over a medium heat for 3-5 minutes.
Once mixture starts to congeal, remove from heat.
Turn mixture out and knead to gain right consistency.

Tips
If you want to make play dough in different colors, add the food coloring at the end of the process. Divide the plain dough into sections, make a well in the middle of the dough and add coloring. Knead until the color is spread through the dough.

To stimulate other senses you can add the following once you have removed the play dough from the heat:
Add essential oils for an attractive fragrance to the play dough.
To make the play dough sparkle, add a handful of micro glitter to the dough to change the appearance.

- According to Dr. Stewart Brown, founder of the national Institute for Play, "If adults can begin to reminisce about their happiest and most memorable moments, they can capture the emotion and visual memories of those moments and begin to connect again to what truly excites them in life. Generally, a person's purest emotional profile— temperament, talents, passions— is reflected in positive play experiences from childhood. If you can understand your own emotional profile when it was in its purest form, you can begin to apply it to your adult life. Going through this process may encourage someone to give serious consideration to shifting to another job that may bring them more joy, or to infuse their current life with those elements that once brought them enlivenment but may have been left behind as they conformed to cultural stereotypes of success."

Talk with your companions about your happiest and most memorable play moments of childhood. How do those times inform your life now? Is there a connection? How can you recapture the excitement that play used to infuse into your life?

B. Journaling Themes

- "There is work that is work and there is play that is play; there is play that is work and work that is play. And in only one of these lies happiness."
— Gelett Burgess

- "Necessity may be the mother of invention, but play is certainly the father."
— Roger von Oech

Make a list of all of the creative activities you have engaged in in the past month. What would you like to do more of?

- "To truly laugh you must be able to take your pain and play with it."
— Charlie Chaplin

- Author Barbara Brannon says that "hidden in our play is the real person that we are. When we honor this person, we open our hearts and our minds to all that is important, even sacred, to us." What does your play tell you about who you are? What is the relationship between what you hold sacred and play?

C. Your Tombstone Inscription
If you had to decide today, what words would you put on your tombstone? You are limited to 3 lines with 20 characters on each line, not including spaces and punctuation.

D. "Play" Collage
Create a collage out of paper, pictures from magazines etc., natural items….that helps you to visually explore what it means to engage in a spiritual practice of play. Use one of the quotes from section B: Journaling

Themes, above if you need a focus. Share your collage with others on the retreat with you after you have finished.
Gather supplies: magazines, found objects, photos, drawings etc. cardboard, wood or other sturdy object to glue the collage pieces onto, glue stick or rubber cement,
Create collage: by positioning cut out or torn pieces of paper onto the cardboard backing to make a unified design. You may want to put a few pieces in place and play with their position before permanently affixing them.
Finishing: after your collage is complete, spray with a shellac to seal or use Mod-Podge sealer. Brush a thin layer of the Mod-Podge over the entire collage using a foam craft brush and then let dry. The Mod-Podge dries clear.

Silence
Spend some time (15-20 minutes minimum) sitting or walking in silence as a way to process the activities and messages of the day.

Closing Ritual — see pages 175-177 for activity choices

Closing Readings — see pages 178-185 for reading choices

Departure

RETREAT NINE - SHADOW

Acknowledging shadow as a spiritual practice means embracing the parts of ourselves that are difficult. It means seeing our whole selves— warts and all. In all of us there occasionally resides anger, jealousy, resentment, envy…even violence. Embracing our shadow or "dark" side means seeing who we are all the time, even when what we are is not pretty to look at— even embarrassing. What parts of myself are difficult to look at? What do I need to acknowledge to be truly whole?

Arrival

If you are retreating alone - use this time to unencumber: turn off phones, acquaint yourself with the space and set up the space the way you will want it for the day, unpack supplies.

If you are retreating in a group, use this time to unencumber as described above PLUS:
Give everyone the opportunity to introduce themselves if appropriate, tell a little about their life at present, and

also tell what items they are putting away for the day so they will be able to be as present as possible during the retreat.

Candle Lighting and Readings
Light a candle and choose several passages to read aloud from the following list as a way to center everyone's attention on the retreat theme.

a. Everything with depth casts a shadow. The shadow is the quality that makes us human. As much as we might wish to reject it in order to try to be "perfect," it is the shadow that gives us our humanity. Embracing the shadow as we move through our lives is what creates our healing or wholeness.
— Cynthia Bischoff

b. Unfortunately there can be no doubt that man is, on the whole, less good than he imagines himself or wants to be. Everyone carries a shadow, and the less it is embodied in the individual's

conscious life, the blacker and denser it is. If an inferiority is conscious, one always has a chance to correct it. Furthermore, it is constantly in contact with other interests, so that it is continually subjected to modifications. But if it is repressed and isolated from consciousness, it never gets corrected.
— Carl Jung

c. On the other hand, the shadow belongs to the wholeness of the personality: the strong man must somewhere be weak, somewhere the clever man must be stupid, otherwise he is too good to be true and falls back on pose and bluff.
— Carl Jung

d. Until we find the courage to love ourselves completely, we will never truly be able to experience the love from those around us. We don't need to guess how we really feel about ourselves at the deepest level. All we have to do is look at how the outer world treats us. If we're not getting the respect, love and appreciation we desire from the outer world, it's more than likely we aren't giving these things to ourselves. This is the benevolence of

the Universe in action. The whole world is a mirror of our own consciousness, and when we make peace with the disowned aspects of ourselves, we make peace with the world.
— Debbie Ford

e. Our shadow is that dark side, the side we would not like to hang out on our clothesline or display on a resume. Yet it is a side that is there, one that can either help us on our life's journey or present a formidable obstacle. If we are wise, we learn to embrace our shadow and see it as a helpful aspect of ourselves, one that can lend depth and beauty to our personality.
— Father Paul Keenan

f. I spent time in Bali a number of years ago, which is a Hindu culture. Over every doorway there are masks of demons to greet you, as if to say: "The shadow lives here, it's part of our life, it's part of our home." That is very different from a Judeo-Christian orientation, which says: "Banish the demons. Keep them as far away as possible. Don't let them in the doorway.
— Connie Zweig

Listening
Allow some time, 30 minutes or more, for each person to go off on their own and process the opening readings. The readings can be written on a large piece of paper for participants to refer to or they can be printed on slips of paper for each person. This time allows for the processing of the words within the hearts and minds of each individual. Participants may want to sit/walk with the readings and then journal about their relationship to the readings and any other insights they notice during this time, or they may want to use their journals as a place in which to have a conversation with themselves and/or the Divine on the topic.

Reflection
"Hearts need education and refinement just as the body needs exercise and moderation." Kabir Helminski, a Sufi sheikh

The activities in this section are intended to give retreat participants the opportunity to have a relationship with the retreat theme…to reflect, to re-create, co-create themselves in the light of their experiences. This can be done in many ways but the ultimate goal is to open oneself to the theme and find ways to incorporate the messages from the listening session into one's being. Participants may want to choose just one activity and spend the allotted time on that one pursuit or they may want to choose a couple of things to spend their time on. Groups may choose to all do the same thing for a time and then come back together to discuss the activity.

A. Small Group Discussion Questions & Activities

- It has been said that illumination is preceded by temptation. Temptations are opportunities to practice. Jesus, Muhammad and Buddha were all tempted as they tried to live out their calling. What temptations do you/have you encountered as you try to live out your calling? What have your temptations taught you?

- "You can only come to the morning through the shadows."
— J.R.R. Tolkien.

Discuss what does this quote means to the members of your group.

B. Journaling Themes

- Carl Jung believed that "in spite of its function as a reservoir for human darkness—or perhaps because of this—the shadow is the seat of creativity." What parts of your shadow side engage your creativity?

- The shadow is the voice of your conscience, reminding you of what you have not forgiven. When you are judging someone else, it shows up to remind you of how you are the same as what you judge. When you make judgments of another, you are projecting your own shadows onto them. You are seeing a reflection of your own inner judgments. What are some things you judge others for or dislike in others, that you need to make peace with in yourself?

- David Zarza says, "I've found in my work as a hypnotherapist that it is very often the case that the very things we feel we are not getting from our world are the very same things that we aren't giving to ourselves." Make a list of the things you need/want that you are not getting from the universe. What can you do differently to embrace these shadow sides?

C. Create a play or write a story using the qualities of your shadow side and your light side as characters
What are their names?
How do they interact with each other? What lessons do they learn from each other? How do they depend on each other?

D. "Shadow" Collage
Create a collage out of paper, pictures from magazines etc., natural items....that helps you to visually explore what it means to engage in a spiritual practice of acknowledging shadow. Use one of the quotes from section B: Journaling Themes, above if

you need a focus. Share your collage with others on the retreat with you after you have finished.

Gather supplies: magazines, found objects, photos, drawings etc. cardboard, wood or other sturdy object to glue the collage pieces onto, glue stick or rubber cement,

Create collage: by positioning cut out or torn pieces of paper onto the cardboard backing to make a unified design. You may want to put a few pieces in place and play with their position before permanently affixing them.

Finishing: after your collage is complete, spray with a shellac to seal or use Mod-Podge sealer. Brush a thin layer of the Mod-Podge over the entire collage using a foam craft brush and then let dry. The Mod-Podge dries clear.

Silence

Spend some time (15-20 minutes minimum) sitting or walking in silence as a way to process the activities and messages of the day.

Closing Ritual — see pages 175-177 for activity choices

Closing Readings — see pages 178-185 for reading choices

Departure

RETREAT TEN - MINDFULNESS

The spiritual practice of mindfulness helps one focus on the specific moment in which they find themselves. Many of us spend much of our time thinking about the past or living in the future. Mindfulness is about living fully in the present moment. It is about intentionally choosing now. It is about feeling what we are feeling right now and not putting off until later what we need to attend to now…truly listen to what or who is in our lives at this very moment. What changes do I need to make in my approach to life to be able to live in the present moment? What is the most important thing to be doing right now?

Arrival

If you are retreating alone - use this time to unencumber: turn off phones, acquaint yourself with the space and set up the space the way you will want it for the day, unpack supplies.

If you are retreating in a group, use this time to unencumber as described above PLUS:

Give everyone the opportunity to introduce themselves if appropriate, tell a little about their life at present, and also tell what items they are putting away for the day so they will be able to be as present as possible during the retreat.

Candle Lighting and Readings
Light a candle and choose several passages to read aloud from the following list as a way to center everyone's attention on the retreat theme.

a. For many years, at great cost, I traveled through many countries, saw the high mountains, the oceans. The only things I did not see were the sparkling dewdrops in the grass just outside my door.
— Rabindranath Tagore

b. In a true you-and-I relationship, we are present mindfully, non-intrusively, the way we are present with things in nature. We do not tell a birch tree it

should be more like an elm. We face it with no agenda, only an appreciation that becomes participation: "I love looking at this birch" becomes "I am this birch" and then "I and this birch are opening to a mystery that transcends and holds us both."
— David Richo

c. Mindfulness is simply being aware of what is happening right now without wishing it were different; enjoying the pleasant without holding on when it changes (which it will); and being with the unpleasant without fearing it will always be this way (which it won't).
— James Baraz

d. Each place is the right place— the place where I now am can be a sacred space.
— Ravi Ravindra

e. I feel we don't really need scriptures. The entire life is an open book, a scripture. Read it. Learn while digging a pit or chopping some wood or cooking some food. If you can't learn from your daily activities, how are you going to understand the scriptures?
— Satchidananda

f. Hence, there is a time to go ahead and a time to stay behind.
There is a time to breathe easy and a time to breathe hard.
There is a time to be vigorous and a time to be gentle.
There is a time to gather and a time to release.
Can you see things as they are
And let them be all on their own?
— Lao-Tzu

g. Some people do not know the difference between mindfulness and concentration. They concentrate on what they're doing, thinking that is being mindful. . . . We can concentrate on what we are doing, but if we are not mindful at the same time, with the ability to reflect on the moment, then if somebody interferes with our concentration, we may blow up, get carried away by anger at being frustrated. If we are mindful, we are aware of the tendency to first concentrate and then to feel anger when something interferes with that concentration. With mindfulness we can concentrate when it is appropriate to do

so and not concentrate when it is appropriate not to do so.
— Ajahn Sumedho

h.   Our suffering stems from ignorance. We react because we do not know what we are doing, because we do not know the reality of ourselves. The mind spends most of the time lost in fantasies and illusions, reliving pleasant or unpleasant experiences and anticipating the future with eagerness or fear. While lost in such cravings or aversions, we are unaware of what is happening now, what we are doing now. Yet surely this moment, now, is the most important for us. We cannot live in the past; it is gone. Nor can we live in the future; it is forever beyond our grasp. We can live only in the present. If we are unaware of our present actions, we are condemned to repeating the mistakes of the past and can never succeed in attaining our dreams for the future. But if we can develop the ability to be aware of the present moment, we can use the past as a guide for ordering our actions in the future, so that we may attain our goal.
— S.N. Goenka

Listening
Allow some time, 30 minutes or more, for each person to go off on their own and process the opening readings. The readings can be written on a large piece of paper for participants to refer to or they can be printed on slips of paper for each person. This time allows for the processing of the words within the hearts and minds of each individual. Participants may want to sit/walk with the readings and then journal about their relationship to the readings and any other insights they notice during this time, or they may want to use their journals as a place in which to have a conversation with themselves and/or the Divine on the topic.

Reflection
"Hearts need education and refinement just as the body needs exercise and moderation." Kabir Helminski, a Sufi sheikh

The activities in this section are intended to give retreat participants the opportunity to have a relationship with the retreat theme…to reflect, to re-

create, co-create themselves in the light of their experiences. This can be done in many ways but the ultimate goal is to open oneself to the theme and find ways to incorporate the messages from the listening session into one's being. Participants may want to choose just one activity and spend the allotted time on that one pursuit or they may want to choose a couple of things to spend their time on. Groups may choose to all do the same thing for a time and then come back together to discuss the activity.

A. Small Group Discussion Questions & Activities

- *The Cheese Sandwich* to read aloud and discuss
"During lunch break at work, the carpenter was getting exasperated. Every time he opened his lunchbox, it was a cheese sandwich. Day after day, week after week, it was the same - a cheese sandwich.
"I am getting sick and tired of this lousy cheese sandwich," complained the carpenter repeatedly. His co-workers gave him some advice; "You don't have

to suffer through a cheese sandwich over and over again.   Tell your wife to make you something different. Be firm with her if you have to."
"But I'm not married," replied the carpenter. By now, puzzled and confused, his colleagues asked, "Then who makes your sandwiches?"
"Well, I do!" replied the carpenter."

- *Counting to Ten*

Find a quiet place to sit. Take several deep centering breaths. Close your eyes and focus your attention on slowly counting to ten. When you get to ten, count back down to one. Continue this for 20 minutes.

If your concentration wanders, start back at number one.

What you may experience….

"One...two...three...I need to go to the grocery store today. Oh, I'm thinking. Okay, back to counting"

"One...two...three...four...this isn't so hard after all... Oh no...that's a thought."

"One...two...three... now I've got it. I'm really concentrating now..."

- *A Sweet Meditation*

Find a place to sit where there are no large distractions. Sit comfortably in a chair, back straight and with both feet on the floor. Breathe deeply in and out three times. Take a sucker out of its wrapper and look at it…its texture, color and size. Put the sucker in your mouth and begin to suck on it and lick it. Attend to its sweetness, texture, shape and any other sensations on the tongue. Continue sucking and licking- but not biting- the sucker. Notice the lollipop's taste, and enjoy it thoroughly until the lollipop is gone.

- *Thich Nhat Hahn's Orange Meditation*

Breathe deeply in and out three times. Pick up an orange and hold it in your hand. Feel its texture. Notice its color. Examine the orange at length.
Begin to peel the orange slowly. Notice the layers of color and texture as you peel it. Notice the oils in the skin. Notice any blemishes or distinguishing characteristics your orange might have.

Take time to smell the orange.
When you have finished peeling the orange, pull off a segment, separating it from the rest of the orange.
Smell the segment.
Bite into it, and concentrate on the orange's flavor. Savor each bite before taking another.
Eat each segment slowly, focusing on all of your senses as you consume the orange.
When the orange is completely eaten, again, breathe deeply in and out three times.
NOTES:
You can do all or part of this meditation with your eyes closed to change your experience.
As you work through this exercise and get distracted, be patient with yourself and just refocus on the orange each time your mind wanders.

- Walking Meditation
In case it isn't obvious, this kind of meditation is done with the eyes open. Choose a place to walk that is away from traffic and on a level surface so that you can walk without paying too much attention to obstacles. You might

begin with a 20-minute walk, although it is up to you how long you walk. It all depends on how much time you have. The purpose of this kind of meditation is to practice staying in the moment and being mindful. This kind of practice is something that can be done on a short walk through a parking lot or on a wooded trail during a lunch break.

As you begin, simply stand in place and feel your feet on the earth. Feel the way your feet balance your body on the ground. As you begin to walk, walk at a slow but normal pace. Be aware of your foot as the heel makes contact with the ground first and then as your foot rolls forward onto the ball, and then as it lifts and travels through the air. Be aware of how your foot feels in your shoe, of your ankles and how relaxed they are, of your calves and knees and thighs as you walk.

Follow your awareness up your body to your neck and then, eventually, to the top of your head, relaxing all of those parts as you continue to walk. Notice your jaw especially…is it relaxed? If not, try to relax it.

Are you bored or content or agitated? Are you feeling happy or sad? Notice your emotions. Is your mind busy, or is it calm? Are you thinking about things unconnected with this practice? Notice these things with no particular judgment and then return to the moment and your walking.

Continue your walk for as long as you have allotted for this practice. You may want to journal about this experience or discuss it with others who are on retreat with you.

B. Journaling Themes
- Spend 10 to 15 minutes just writing down whatever comes into your mind, no matter how silly or strange. What am I feeling and thinking right now?

- Notice 5 things you can hear or see and record them in your journal

- Write about 3 good things in your life.

C. "Mindfulness" Collage
Create a collage out of paper, pictures from magazines etc., natural items….that helps you to visually

explore what it means to engage in a spiritual practice of acknowledging shadow. Use one of the quotes from section B: Journaling Themes, above if you need a focus. Share your collage with others on the retreat with you after you have finished.

Gather supplies: magazines, found objects, photos, drawings etc. cardboard, wood or other sturdy object to glue the collage pieces onto, glue stick or rubber cement,

Create collage: by positioning cut out or torn pieces of paper onto the cardboard backing to make a unified design. You may want to put a few pieces in place and play with their position before permanently affixing them.

Finishing: after your collage is complete, spray with a shellac to seal or use Mod-Podge sealer. Brush a thin layer of the Mod-Podge over the entire collage using a foam craft brush and then let dry. The Mod-Podge dries clear.

Silence

Spend some time (15-20 minutes minimum) sitting or walking in silence as a way to process the activities and messages of the day.

Closing Ritual — see pages 175-177 for activity choices

Closing Readings — see pages 178-185 for reading choices

Departure

RETREAT ELEVEN — LISTENING

The practice of listening is not only about others, it is also about listening to one's self, the Divine, the universe. It is about taking the time to really hear what is being "said" or not being said. It has as components, the practices of hospitality, openness, connection and silence. What keeps me from truly listening? What would it mean to the quality of my relationships if I listened twice as much as I spoke?

Arrival
If you are retreating alone - use this time to unencumber: turn off phones, acquaint yourself with the space and set up the space the way you will want it for the day, unpack supplies.

If you are retreating in a group, use this time to unencumber as described above PLUS:
Give everyone the opportunity to introduce themselves if appropriate, tell a little about their life at present, and also tell what items they are putting away for the day so they will be able to

be as present as possible during the retreat.

Candle Lighting and Readings
Light a candle and choose several passages to read aloud from the following list as a way to center everyone's attention on the retreat theme.

a. One friend, one person who is truly understanding, who takes the trouble to listen to us, can change our whole outlook on the world.
— Dr. E. H. Mayo

b. To listen fully means to pay close attention to what is being said beneath the words. You listen not only to the 'music,' but to the essence of the person speaking. You listen not only for what someone knows, but for what he or she is. Ears operate at the speed of sound, which is far slower than the speed of light the eyes take in. Generative listening is the art of developing deeper silences in yourself, so you can slow our mind's hearing to your ears' natural

speed, and hear beneath the words to their meaning.
— Peter Senge

c. The greatest compliment that was ever paid me was when one asked me what I thought, and attended to my answer.
— Henry David Thoreau

d. Listening, not imitation, may be the sincerest form of flattery.
— Dr Joyce Brothers

e. An essential part of true listening is the discipline of bracketing, the temporary giving up or setting aside of one's own prejudices, frames of reference and desires so as to experience as far as possible the speaker's world from the inside, step in inside his or her shoes. This unification of speaker and listener is actually and extension and enlargement of ourselves, and new knowledge is always gained from this. Moreover, since true listening involves bracketing, a setting aside of the self, it also temporarily involves a total acceptance of the other. Sensing this acceptance, the speaker will fell less and less

vulnerable and more and more inclined to open up the inner recesses of his or her mind to the listener. As this happens, speaker and listener begin to appreciate each other more and more, and the duet dance of love is begun again.
— M. Scott Peck

f. The more faithfully you listen to the voices within you, the better you will hear what is sounding outside.
— Dag Hammarskjold

g. When we talk about understanding, surely it takes place only when the mind listens completely — the mind being your heart, your nerves, your ears- when you give your whole attention to it.
— Jiddu Krishnamurti

h. For listening is the act of entering the skin of the other and wearing it for a time as if it were our own. Listening is the gateway to understanding.
 — David Spangler

Listening
Allow some time, 30 minutes or more, for each person to go off on their own and process the opening readings. The readings can be written on a large piece of paper for participants to refer to or they can be printed on slips of paper for each person. This time allows for the processing of the words within the hearts and minds of each individual. Participants may want to sit/walk with the readings and then journal about their relationship to the readings and any other insights they notice during this time, or they may want to use their journals as a place in which to have a conversation with themselves and/or the Divine on the topic.

Reflection
"Hearts need education and refinement just as the body needs exercise and moderation." Kabir Helminski, a Sufi sheikh

The activities in this section are intended to give retreat participants the opportunity to have a relationship with the retreat theme…to reflect, to re-

create, co-create themselves in the light of their experiences. This can be done in many ways but the ultimate goal is to open oneself to the theme and find ways to incorporate the messages from the listening session into one's being. Participants may want to choose just one activity and spend the allotted time on that one pursuit or they may want to choose a couple of things to spend their time on. Groups may choose to all do the same thing for a time and then come back together to discuss the activity.

A. Small Group Discussion Questions & Activities

- Share with others in your small group stories of times when you experienced difficulty really hearing what someone else was trying to say, about times when you felt unheard and about times when you felt that you were truly listened to.

- Spend 5 minutes, as a group, just listening to the world around you. After 5 minutes, discuss what you heard.
Try it again for 8 minutes and then 10 minutes.

B. Journaling Themes

- *Lectio Divina- Holy Reading*: This kind of reading encourages us to not just read the words of a passage but to listen to what the passage is trying to say to us. It involves cultivating the ability to listen deeply, to hear "with the ear of our hearts" according to St. Benedict.

Choose a scripture passage, poem, or other short reading to contemplate and journal about.

Read through the passage silently and then aloud.

Spend some time thinking and/or journaling about the passage. What is it saying to you? What questions do you have for the passage?

Put yourself into the passage as one of the characters or situations. How are you affected by the context of the passage? How does changing your point of view change the story?

Read the passage again and listen for any final revelation.

Suggested Passages:

From the Jewish Tradition:

Psalm 23
(New International Version)

The LORD is my shepherd, I lack nothing.
He makes me lie down in green pastures,
he leads me beside quiet waters,
he refreshes my soul.
He guides me along the right paths for his name's sake.
Even though I walk
through the darkest valley,
I will fear no evil,
for you are with me;
your rod and your staff,
they comfort me.

You prepare a table before me in the presence of my enemies.
You anoint my head with oil;
my cup overflows.
Surely your goodness and love will follow me
all the days of my life,

and I will dwell in the house of the Lord forever.

From the Christian Tradition:

Matthew 5:3-12
(New International Version)

The Beatitudes

Blessed are the poor in spirit,
for theirs is the kingdom of heaven.
Blessed are those who mourn,
for they will be comforted.
Blessed are the meek,
for they will inherit the earth.
Blessed are those who hunger and thirst for righteousness,
for they will be filled.
Blessed are the merciful,
for they will be shown mercy.
Blessed are the pure in heart,
for they will see God.
Blessed are the peacemakers,
for they will be called children of God.
Blessed are those who are persecuted because of righteousness,
for theirs is the kingdom of heaven.

Blessed are you when people insult you, persecute you and falsely say all kinds of evil against you because of me. Rejoice and be glad, because great is your reward in heaven, for in the same way they persecuted the prophets who were before you.

From the Buddhist Tradition:

The Four Immeasurables
May all beings have happiness and its causes,
May they never have suffering nor its causes;
May they constantly dwell in joy transcending sorrow;
May they dwell in equal love for both near and far.

May I protect the helpless and the poor,
May I be a lamp,
For those who need your Light,
May I be a bed for those who need rest,
and guide all seekers to the Other Shore.
May all find happiness through my actions,

and let no one suffer because of me.
Whether they love or hate me,
Whether they hurt or wrong me.

From the Hindu Tradition:

Morning Prayer
May all in this world be happy,
may they be healthy,
may they be comfortable
and never miserable.

May the rain come down in the proper time,
may the earth yield plenty of corn,
may the country be free from war,
may the Brahmans be secure.

A Prayer for Peace
O God, lead us from the unreal to the Real.
O God lead us from darkness to light.
O God, lead us from death to immortality.
Shanti*, Shanti, Shanti unto all.
O Lord God almighty,
May there be peace in celestial regions.
May there be peace on earth.
May the waters be appeasing.

May herbs be wholesome, and
May trees and plants bring peace to all.
May all beneficent beings bring peace to us.
May your Vedic Law propagate peace all through the world.
May all things be a source of peace to us.
And may your peace itself bestow peace on all, and
May that peace come to me also.
*(Shanti=Peace)

- Write about times when you experienced difficulty really hearing what someone else was trying to say, about times when you felt unheard and about times when you felt that you were truly listened to.

C. "Listening" Collage
Create a collage out of paper, pictures from magazines etc., natural items....that helps you to visually explore what it means to engage in a spiritual practice of listening. Use one of the quotes from section B: Journaling Themes, above if you need a focus.

Share your collage with others on the retreat with you after you have finished.
Gather supplies: magazines, found objects, photos, drawings etc. cardboard, wood or other sturdy object to glue the collage pieces onto, glue stick or rubber cement,
Create collage: by positioning cut out or torn pieces of paper onto the cardboard backing to make a unified design. You may want to put a few pieces in place and play with their position before permanently affixing them.
Finishing: after your collage is complete, spray with a shellac to seal or use Mod-Podge sealer. Brush a thin layer of the Mod-Podge over the entire collage using a foam craft brush and then let dry. The Mod-Podge dries clear.

Silence
Spend some time (15-20 minutes minimum) sitting or walking in silence as a way to process the activities and messages of the day.

Closing Ritual — see pages 175-177 for activity choices

Closing Readings — see pages 178-185 for reading choices

Departure

RETREAT TWELVE - JUSTICE

Justice as a spiritual practice means working to insure that the world is as equitable as possible for as many living creatures as possible. It means acknowledging the dignity of others, even when we don't agree with them. It means cultivating just relationships. And, justice seeks to foster and nurture a deeper connection between the self and the world in which we live. What are the hallmarks of a life grounded in equity and justice.

Arrival

If you are retreating alone - use this time to unencumber: turn off phones, acquaint yourself with the space and set up the space the way you will want it for the day, unpack supplies.

If you are retreating in a group, use this time to unencumber as described above PLUS:
Give everyone the opportunity to introduce themselves if appropriate, tell a little about their life at present, and

also tell what items they are putting away for the day so they will be able to be as present as possible during the retreat.

Candle Lighting and Readings
Light a candle and choose several passages to read aloud from the following list as a way to center everyone's attention on the retreat theme.

a. We must not, in trying to think about how we can make a difference, ignore the small daily differences we can make, which, over time, add up to big differences we cannot foresee.
— Marian Wright Edelman

b. There can be little growth in holiness without growth in a sense of social justice.
— Edward Hays

c. Do not be surprised or scandalized by the sinful and the tragic. Do what you can to be peace and to do justice, but

never expect or demand perfection on this earth.
— Richard Rohr

d. Never doubt that a small group of thoughtful, committed people can change the world. Indeed, it is the only thing that ever has.
— Margaret Mead

e. If you are neutral in situations of injustice, you have chosen the side of the oppressor. If an elephant has its foot on the tail of a mouse and you say that you are neutral, the mouse will not appreciate your neutrality.
— Archbishop Desmond Tutu

f. Until the great mass of the people shall be filled with the sense of responsibility for each other's welfare, social justice can never be attained.
— Helen Keller

g. Where justice is denied, where poverty is enforced, where ignorance prevails, and where any one class is made to feel that society is an organized conspiracy to oppress, rob and degrade

them, neither persons nor property will be safe.
— Frederick Douglass

Listening
Allow some time, 30 minutes or more, for each person to go off on their own and process the opening readings. The readings can be written on a large piece of paper for participants to refer to or they can be printed on slips of paper for each person. This time allows for the processing of the words within the hearts and minds of each individual. Participants may want to sit/walk with the readings and then journal about their relationship to the readings and any other insights they notice during this time, or they may want to use their journals as a place in which to have a conversation with themselves and/or the Divine on the topic.

Reflection
"Hearts need education and refinement just as the body needs exercise and moderation." Kabir Helminski, a Sufi sheikh

The activities in this section are intended to give retreat participants the opportunity to have a relationship with the retreat theme…to reflect, to re-create, co-create themselves in the light of their experiences. This can be done in many ways but the ultimate goal is to open oneself to the theme and find ways to incorporate the messages from the listening session into one's being. Participants may want to choose just one activity and spend the allotted time on that one pursuit or they may want to choose a couple of things to spend their time on. Groups may choose to all do the same thing for a time and then come back together to discuss the activity.

A. Small Group Discussion Questions & Activities

Discuss the following in your small group:

Can justice best be achieved through reform or revolution? Are you more of a reformer or a revolutionary? Share a

personal story that illustrates your answer.
How does your understanding of pursuing justice change if it comes out of a sense of freedom versus obligation?

Erich Fromm suggests that in addition to desiring to be free, it is human nature to desire someone or something to which we can submit—and therefore avoid taking responsibility for our actions. What are your thoughts on this? Share a personal story that illustrates, or refutes, Fromm's idea about submission.

It has been said that the only way to liberate the world and ourselves is by joining together and marching. Who are the people with whom you already march? With whom would it be strategic/prudent for you to march in order to bring about a just world?

It has been argued that religion is:
(a) sometimes a strong cause for violence (the violence is "really about religion")

(b) sometimes a weak cause (religion is "an ingredient…that ratchets up the conflict")
(c) conversely, sometimes a cause for peace.
Can you think of examples to illustrate each?

B. Journaling Themes

- Erich Fromm suggests that in addition to desiring to be free, it is human nature to desire someone or something to which we can submit—and therefore avoid taking responsibility for our actions. What are your thoughts on this? Write in your journal a personal story that illustrates, or refutes, Fromm's idea about submission.

- Can justice best be achieved through reform or revolution? Are you more of a reformer or a revolutionary? Share a personal story that illustrates your answer.

- It has been said that the only way to liberate the world and ourselves is by joining together and marching. Who are the people with whom you already march? With whom would it be strategic/prudent for you to march in order to bring about a just world?

C. Songs of Justice

Sing or listen to peace and justice songs with others as you sit or walk.

Some suggestions:

- If I Had a Hammer
- Blowing in the Wind
- Where Have All the Flowers Gone?
- One Tin Soldier
- I'd Like to Teach the World to Sing

D. "Justice" Collage
Create a collage out of paper, pictures from magazines etc., natural items….that helps you to visually explore what it means to engage in a spiritual practice of justice. Use one of the quotes from section B: Journaling Themes, above if you need a focus.

Share your collage with others on the retreat with you after you have finished.
<u>Gather supplies</u>: magazines, found objects, photos, drawings etc. cardboard, wood or other sturdy object to glue the collage pieces onto, glue stick or rubber cement,
<u>Create collage:</u> by positioning cut out or torn pieces of paper onto the cardboard backing to make a unified design. You may want to put a few pieces in place and play with their position before permanently affixing them.
<u>Finishing:</u> after your collage is complete, spray with a shellac to seal or use Mod-Podge sealer. Brush a thin layer of the Mod-Podge over the entire collage using a foam craft brush and then let dry. The Mod-Podge dries clear.

Silence

Spend some time (15-20 minutes minimum) sitting or walking in silence as a way to process the activities and messages of the day.

Closing Ritual — see pages 175-177 for activity choices

_____

Closing Readings — see pages 178-185 for reading choices

_____

Departure

Author Index

The first number corresponds to the twelve sections of quotes.
The second number corresponds to the numbered quotes in that section.

Retreat references are for the quotes in the Retreats section under the "Candle Lightings and Readings" heading.

A

Bluejay Adametz: 10:12,
Anne Adams: 11:3,
Douglas Adams: 11:28,
Jane Addams: 6:15,
Felix Adler: 5:12, 9:13, 12:10,
Imam Al— Haddad: 9:5,
Ruben Alves: 1:22,
James Allen: 10:31,
Marian Anderson: 7:22,
Maya Angelou: 1:28, 2:9, 7:4,
on the tomb of an Anglican Bishop in Westminster Abbey: 3:20,
Karen Armstrong: 7:15,
Jean Arp: Retreat 6-f,
Isaac Asimov; 3:9,
Francis of Assisi: 1:17, 6:17, 11:10,
St. Augustine: 12:17, Retreat 7-c,
Teresa of Avila: 1:7, 11:8,

B
Satya Sai Baba: 4:18,
Richard Bach: 2:7, 3:13, 7:13,
Elsa Joy Bailey: Retreat 1-e,
James Baldwin: 7:25, 10:13,
James Baraz: Retreat 10-c,
Raymond Charles Barker: 4:11,
Basil the Great: 10:26,
George Kimmich Beach: 12:3,
Melody Beattie: 4:19,
Henry Ward Beecher: 9:19, Retreat 5-a,
Mark L. Belletini: p.181,
Robert Benson: 11:4,
Isaiah Berlin: 11:15,
Yogi Berra: 12:30,
Daniel Berrigan: 3:7, 9:30,
Wendell Berry: 6:9,
Bhagavad Gita: 3:2, 3:30, 7:21,
Cynthia Bischoff: Retreat 9-a,
Algernon Black: 2:18, 5:11,
Black Elk: 1:19, 3:21,
Barbara Bloom: 9:31,
J. Allen Boone: 5:1,
Daniel J. Boorstin: 6:19,
Joan Borysenko: 4:17,
Kay Boyle: 12:14,
Ray Bradbury: 3:18, 9:21, 10:7,
Sarah Ban Breathnach: 6:13,
Tom Brokaw: 10:28,
Dr Joyce Brothers: Retreat 11-d,
H. Jackson Brown: 6:3,

Robert McAfee Brown: 5:9,
Jesse Browner: Retreat 2-b,
Beatrice Bruteau: 2:29,
from the Buddhist tradition: 5:21, 10:25,
Martin Buber: 2:3,
Frederick Buechner: 9:15,
John Burroughs: 9:1,
Eric Butterworth: 5:13,
Witter Bynner: 11:22,

C

Joseph Campbell: 5:16,
Albert Camus: 4:11, 6:14,
Norbert Capek: 5:4,
Robert Farrer Capon: Retreat 7-d,
Fritjof Capra: 4:3,
David Carradine: 2:19,
Carlo Carretto: 11:27,
Lewis Carroll: 8:7,
Jimmy Carter: 1:10,
Rosalynn Carter: 10:22,
George Washington Carver: 11:2,
Willa Cather: 6:28,
from the Cherokee tradition: 2:13,
Gilbert K. Chesterton: Retreat 4-b,
Chief Joseph: 10:29,
Chief Seattle: Retreat 3-d,
Forrest Church: 9:14,
Pema Chodron: Retreat 1-b,
William Cleary: page 236,
Paul Coehlo: 11:7,

Confucius: 6:10, 10:30, 11:1,
Norman Cousins: 10:19,
Stephen Covey: 2:16, 4:14, Retreat 4-f,
Harvey Cox: 9:17,
Thomas Cullinan: 11:12,

D
The Dalai Lama: 11:29, Retreat 3-b,
Ram Dass: 7:27, 10:27,
Richard Dawkins: Retreat 5-d,
Dorothy Day: 7:6, 9:10,
Frederik W. de Klerk: 7:9,
Charles de Lint: 8:30,
Anthony de Mello: 12:15,
Agnes De Mille: 10:6,
Antoine De Saint-Exupery: 2:4, 8:2, 12:25, Retreat 3-e,
Eugene V. Debs: 3:22,
Johnny Depp: 8:12,
The Dhammapada: 12:29,
Emily Dickinson: 4:6,
Annie Dillard: 9:12,
Fyodor Dostoyevsky: 2:21,
Frederick Douglass: 6:20, 9:16, Retreat 12-g,
Rita Dove: Retreat 4-c,
Charles Dubois: 2:12,
Henry Drummond: 2:6,

E

Eknath Easwaran: 6:18, 7:11,
Meister Eckhart: 9:2,
Marian Wright Edelman: 4:28, Retreat 12-a,
Albert Einstein: 1:30, 2:20, 3:1, 3:31, 4:13, 4:22, 5:5, 7:7, 8:9, 12:31, Retreat 3-c, Retreat 4-d, Retreat 7-a,
T. S. Eliot: 2:14,
Susan Ely: Retreat 2-e,
Ralph Waldo Emerson: 1:24, 2:1, 5:31, 6:4, 7:23, 12:1, 12:5, 12:21, Retreat 2-d,
Epictetus: 5:10,
Susan Ertz: 3:12,

F

William Faulkner: Retreat 5-b,
Ludwig Feuerbach: 6:22,
James Finley: 4:21,
Debbie Ford: Retreat 9-d,
Sam Walter Foss: Retreat 2-a,
Robert H. Frank: 12:22,
Victor Frankl: 4:12, 5:30,
James Dillet Freeman: 8:17,
James A. Froude: 5:27,
Robert Fulghum: 9:8, Retreat 4-e,
Margaret Fuller: 9:20,
R. Buckminster Fuller: 10:8,

G
Galileo: 5:2,
Indira Gandhi: 5:29,
Mahatma Gandhi: 3:11, 4:25, 8:16, 8:22, 11:18, 12:19, Retreat 3-g, Retreat 6-b,
Kahlil Gibran: 8:18, 10:4,
Elizabeth Gilbert: 7:30, 12:27, 11:31,
Richard S. Gilbert: 9:25,
Charlotte Perkins Gilman: 6:30,
S.N. Goenka: Retreat 10-h,
Ellen Goodman: 12:11,
Sarah Leah Grafstein: 3:23,
Karl Groos: Retreat 8-d,

H
Thich Nhat Hanh: 1:29, 2:31, 10:2, Retreat 7-f,
Dag Hammarskjold: 1:20, 11:16, Retreat 11-f,
Willis Harman: 5:3,
Andrew Harvey: Retreat 1-f,
from Tales of the Hasidim: 10:16, 10:20,
Katherine Butler Hathaway: 9:26,
Edward Hays: Retreat 12-b,
Heraclitus: Retreat 8-a,
Friedrich Otto Hertz: 6:5,
Abraham Heschel: 1:18, 7:29,
Hermann Hesse: 8:20,
from the Hindu tradition: 2:8, 2:28, 5:6, 12:12, 12:16,
Eric Hoffer: 4:27, 11:25, 12:28,

Kent Hoffman: Retreat 3-f,
Oliver Wendell Holmes: 3:29,
Father Daniel Homan: Retreat 2-g,
bell hooks: 6:27, 7:28,
Roger Housden: Retreat 1-g,
Jane Howard: 3:17,
James C. Howell: 3:25,
Elbert Hubbard: 12:2,
Victor Hugo: 6:24,
Johan Huizing: Retreat 8-g,
Basil Hume: 7:31,
Aldous Huxley: 7:24,

I
From the Irish tradition: 11:6,

J
William James: 11:19,
Thomas Jefferson: 6:31,
from the Jewish tradition: 10:24,
Steve Jobs: 12:26,
Samuel Johnson: 3:5,
E. Stanley Jones: 7:5,
John Henry Jowett: Retreat 5-f,
Sara Covin Juengst: Retreat 2-f,
Carl Jung: 6:23, 12:4, Retreat 9-b,
Retreat 9-c,

K
Mordecai M. Kaplan: p.183,
Immanuel Kant: Retreat 7-e,

Kurt Kauter: 4:26,
Sam Keen; 3:10,
Father Paul Keenan: Retreat 9-e,
Helen Keller: 4:9, 10:5, Retreat 12-f,
Martin Luther King, Jr: 3:6, 4:1, 7:19,
John Fitzgerald Kennedy: Retreat 5-c,
Robert F Kennedy: 2:2, 7:20,
Ken Keyes, Jr: 10:14,
Sue Monk Kidd: 1:4, 8:14,
Barbara Kingsolver: 9:9,
Anita Koddick: 7:17,
Jiddu Krishnamurti: Retreat 11-g,
Elisabeth Kűbler-Ross: 8:31, Retreat 6-c,
Harold Kushner; 6:26, Retreat 5-g,

L
Anne Lamott: 11:30, 12:9
Lao-Tzu: 6:7, 6:29, 9:7, Retreat 10-f,
Abraham Lincoln: 3:8,
Ann Landers: 2:15,
Madeleine L'Engle: 2:25, 8:25,
Henry Wadsworth Longfellow: 5:14, 10:17,
Barry Lopez: 4:8,
Max Lucado: 10:21, 11:11,
Lucretious: 9:18,

M
Nisargadatta Maharaj: 1:14,
Ramana Maharshi: 1:11,

Dr. E. H. Mayo: Retreat 11-a,
Robert McCloskey: 7:12,
Susan McHenry: 5:20,
Abraham Maslow: 6:25, Retreat 8-c,
Margaret Mead: Retreat 12-d,
Herman Melville: 3:15,
Thomas Merton: 3:16, 8:23, ,
James A Michener: 4;23,
Henry Miller: 4:4,
Peter Minard: Retreat 6-g,
Thomas Moore: Retreat 4-a,
Mark Morrison-Reed: 5:8,
John Muir: 5:24,
Susan Murphy: 2:10,

N
Rebbe Nachman of Breslov: Retreat 6-a,
Reinhold Neibuhr: 6:11,
Kent Nerburn: 3:14,
Friedrich Nietzsche: 4:7,
Anaïs Nin: 1:13, 5:18, Retreat 7-g,
Arthur Darby Nock: 11:14,
Kathleen Norris: Retreat 2-c,
Henri J. M. Nouwen: 11:26,
Cathy Nutbrown: Retreat 8-h,

O
Sandra Day O' Connor: 4:15,
John O'Donohue: 11:9,
Mary Oliver: 3:28, 8:11,

Emma Restall Orr: Retreat 3-a,

P
Chuck Palahniuk: 8:8,
Parker Palmer: 1:6, 6:12, 11:13,
Rebecca Ann Parker: 7:2,
Christopher Paolini: 9:6,
Ibu Patel: 12:20,
Kenneth L. Patton: 10:15,
Randy Pausch: 8:13,
M. Scott Peck: 2:26, 4:30, 6:8, Retreat 11-e,
William Penn: 8:3,
Thomas G. Pettepiece: 11:20,
Jean Piaget: Retreat 8-e,
Jodi Picoult: 8:15,
Robert M. Pirsig: 4:5,
Plato: 3:3, Retreat 8-b,
Lonni Gollins Pratt: Retreat 2-g,
Marcel Proust: 1:26,

Q
Anna Quindlen: 8:26,
Michael Quoist: 1:1,

R
Mary Ann Radmacher: 8:4,
Ramakrishna: 1:15, 2:17, 9:3,
Ravi Ravindra: Retreat 10-d,
Marie Beyon (M.B.)Ray: 5:17, 11:5,
Christopher Reeve: 1:16,

Rachel Naomi Remen: 7:1,
David Richo: Retreat 10-b,
Rainer Maria Rilke: 8:10,
Theodore Roethke: 6:2,
Richard Rohr: Retreat 12-c,
Theodore Roosevelt: 3:4,
Mark I. Rosen: 6:16,
L. A. Rouchefolicauld: 2:27,
Carl T. Rowan: 7:8,
Rumi: 4:31, 9:28,
Bertrand Russell: 9:29,

S

Abu Sa'id: 10:3,
Mitsugi Saotome: 3:26,
May Sarton: 9:24,
Satchidananda: Retreat 10-e,
Albert Schweitzer: 8:28, 12:18, Retreat 5-e,
Anne B. Sekel: 12:23,
Seneca: 4:23,
Peter Senge: Retreat 11-b,
Rabbi Rami Shapiro: 1:12, 11:17,
George Bernard Shaw: 8:21, 12:13,
Shel Silverstein: 1:25,
Adlin Sinclair: 8:6,
Charles L. Slattery: 4:20,
Arthur Solomon: 7:26,
Robert C. Solomon: Retreat 7-b,
Alfred D. Souza: 2:22,
David Spangler: Retreat 11-h,

Gerry Spence: 6:1,
Paula Underwood Spencer: 1:9,
W.A. Spooner: 8:19,
Charles H. Spurgeon: 11:24,
Ben Stallings: p. 182,
Adlai Stevens: 8:1,
from the Sufi tradition: 2:23, 10:18,
Ajahn Sumedho: Retreat 10-g,
Sun Bear: 5:22,

T
Rabindranath Tagore: 5:25, Retreat 10-a,
from the Talmud: 1:8,
from the Tao Te Ching: 8:29, Retreat 1-a,
P. Teilhard de Chardin: 12:7,
Mother Teresa: 12:24,
Terma Collective: Retreat 1-c,
Franklin Thomas: 5:19,
Henry David Thoreau: 1:23, 5:15, 6:6, 9:27, Retreat 11-c,
Eckhart Tolle: Retreat 6-e,
Leo Tolstoy: 8:24,
Jacob Trapp: 1:21,
Desmond Tutu: 7:3, 9:23, 10:10, Retreat 12-e,
Mark Twain: 5:7, 6:21,
Chuang Tzu: 1:3,

U
Universal Peace Prayer: 12:6,
from The Upanishads: 4:2,

V
Henry Van Dyke: 2:30,
Vincent Van Gogh: 2:24, 10:11,
Voltaire: 5:26,

W
Benjamin Wallace: 9:22, p.179, p.182,
Andy Warhol: 1:31,
Max Warren: 4:29,
Lila Watson: 7:18,
John Welwood: Retreat 1-d,
Alan Wilson Watts: 9:4,
Simone Weil: 3:24,
Robert T. Weston: 10:9,
Meg Wheatley: p. 178,
E. B. White: 5:28, 8:27,
Alfred North Whitehead: 9:11,
Harold Whitman: 7:10,
Macrina Wiederkehr: Retreat 6-d,
Elie Wiesel: 3:27,
Oscar Wilde: 10:23,
Tad Williams: 11:23,
Edward O. Wilson: 10:1,
Maria Wilson: p. 184,
Walter Wink: 7:14,
D.W. Winnicott: Retreat 8-f,

Y

Whitney Young: 2:11,
Lin Yutang: 5:23,

Z

Gary Zukov: 2:5,
Connie Zweig: Retreat 9-f,

Subject Index

The first number corresponds to the twelve sections of quotes.
The second number corresponds to the numbered quotes in that section.

A
Acceptance: 12:18,
Actions: 8:22, 12:21, 12:22,
Adventure: 3:13,
After-life: 11:28,
Anger: 7:11, 10:27,
Answers: 1:4, 2:26, 2:27, 8:10,
Attention: 2:5,
Attitude: 5:30,
Awareness: 4:3,

B
The Battle Within: 2:13,
Beauty: 2:18, 9:31,
Becoming Alive: 7:10,
Being/Discovering Yourself: 1:8, 1:11, 2:12, 2:19, 2:24, 3:24, 6:29, 8:26, 12:27,
Beliefs: 8:22, 8:25, 12:20,
Blindness: 12:19,
The Body: 12:25,
The Brave: 7:21,
Broken: 9:31,
Brother's Keeper: 3:22,

Building: 2:4, 11:7,
Burdens: 10:24,

C
Ceremony: 5:22,
Change: 8:17, 11:12, 12:13,
Changing the World: 3:20, 7:6, 8:6, 10:30, 11:2,
Chaos: 10:1,
Character: 5:27, 6:3, 10:29, 12:23,
Choices: 2:8, 2:13, 3:22, 3:24, 3:28, 4:8, 5:30, 7:26, 11:2,
Closed Doors: 10:5,
Communion: 9:1,
Community: 2:28, 3:17, 5:9, 6:8, 6:26, 10:15, 11:15, 12:3, 12:9,
Compassion: 3:31, 7:16, 7:29, 7:30, 8:29, 10:2,
Complexity: 4:30,
Connectedness: 3:15, 3:17, 3:20, 4:1, 5:3, 5:24, 5:25, 6:6, 7:4, 7:18, 7:27, 7:30, 8:28, 9:27, 9:28, 10:4, 10:8, 11:3,
Contradiction: 4:8,
Control: 11:14,
Cooking: 9:24,
Cosmic Orchestra: 5:1,
Courage: 1:7, 7:20, 8:4, 11:9, 11:21,

D
The Dance: 4:7, 6:9,

Darkness: 8:31,
Dealing with Insults: 1:2,
Death: 8:8, 9:14, 10:7, 12:25,
Decisions: 3:4, 3:23, 4:11,
Desires: 10:27,
Destiny: 8:22, 10:6, 12:21,
Differences: 5:11, 5:12, 5:19,
Difficult People: 6:16,
Discomfort: 2:26,
Diversity: 10:12,
Doing the Impossible: 6:17,
Doing your Duty: 1:15, 3:4, 3:23, 6:30, 7:16, 7:26, 9:23,
Domination: 7:28,
Done and Undone: 5:23,
Doubt: 10:9,
Dreams: 1:16,

E
Empathy: 7:16,
Enemies: 10:17,
The Environment: 10:1,
Equilibrium: 10:1,
Everyday Living: 9:24,
Evil: 2:13,
Excellence: 4:24,
Eye for an Eye: 12:19,

F
Failure: 12:12,
Faith: 2:25, 6:11,

Family: 3:17,
Fear: 11:9,
Our Flame: 8:28,
Flight: 6:24,
Forgiveness: 6:11, 7:21, 10:19,
Freedom: 5:30,
Friendship: 4:20, 5:28, 12:5,
The Future: 1:1, 1:22, 12:11,

G
Garden: 5:15, 11:7,
Getting Along: 4:27,
Getting What We Need: 6:12,
Giving: 5:6, 9:30 (of ourselves),
God: 1:15 (keeping your mind on God), 2:2, 2:17, 2:23, 5:13, 6:5, 6:31, 7:31 12:9 (reflections of God), 9:3, 9:13 (hidden in me), 11:6, 11:8, 11:24 (serving God), 11:30, 12:7,
Golden Rule: 8:19,
Good: 2:13, 6:15, 12:18 (doing good),
Grace: 7:2,
Gratitude: 4:19,
Growth: 5:18, 6:25, 12:13,
Growing Old: 5:9,

H
Habits: 8:22,
Happiness: 4:16, 6:14, 8:5, 7:30, 8:16, 9:21, 10:5, 11:25, 12:22,

Harbor: 4:23,
(No) Harm: 3:30,
Harmony: 3:26,
Hate: 2:8, 7:21, 10:13, 11:30,
Healing: 12:4,
Heart: 5:21, 9:1, 12:9
Hearing: 7:12, 9:1,
Hell: 1:12, 9:12,
Helping Others: 2:1, 2:28, 6:21, 12:16,
Heroes: 3:10,
History: 7:25, 12:14,
Hoarding: 10:26,
Holy: 2:3, 4:29,
Home: 11:23,
Honoring the Dead: 2:20,
Hope; 6:11, 9:9, 9:30,
Hopeless: 9:10,
Hospitality: 11:26,
Hunger: 9:30,

I

Ideas/Ideals: 5:4, 8:21,
Ignorance: 6:19,
Illusion: 6:12, 6:19,
Imagination: 9:8,
Immortality: 3:12,
Improving the World: 4:5, 8:27, 9:23, 11:10,
Indifference: 3:27,
Injustice: 7:6, 7:8, 10:10,
Inspiration: 3:10, 8:2, 8:3,

J
Jesus: 1:2,
The Jewel in Our Hearts: 6:18,
The Journey: 10:15, 10:16, 11:23,
Joy: 3:26,
Judging: 5:14,
Justice: 2:23, 3:6, 3:7, 12:3,

K
Keeping a Person Down: 7:22,
Kindness: 3:5, 4:20, 7:11, 11:29,
Knowledge: 6:6, 9:8, 9:20,
Knowing: 5:10,
Knowing Others: 3:18, 10:2,

L
Laughing: 4:7,
Leaders: 10:22,
Learning: 8:9,
Letting Go: 1:6, 2:29, 4:4, 6:29, 8:11, 11:31, 12:11,
Liberation: 7:18,
Life: 3:26, 3:28, 4:8, 4:11, 5:25, 5:31, 6:9, 6:13 (authentic), 7:13 (mission in life), 8:19, 9:25 (messiness), 11:13, 12:27 (life's passion),
Light: 8:31, 9:5, 9:20, 10:16,
Listening: 1:20, 1:25, 7:1, 8:20,
(Advice for) Living: 2:6, 2:7, 2:9, 2:17, 3:1, 3:4, 4:6, 4:11, 4:23, 5:17, 6:13,

7:13, 8:23, 10:4, 11:5, 11:6, 11:19, 12:1, 12:7, 12:8, 12:26, 12:27, 12:28, 12:31,
Lord's Prayer: 3:7,
Losing Yourself: 10:18,
Love: 1:14, 1:22, 2:6, 2:21, 3:11, 3:16, 4:17, 4:21, 6:11, 6:27, 6:28, 7:6, 7:21, 7:28, 7:29, 8:12, 9:8, 10:2, 10:4 (of your neighbor), 10:14,
Luggage & Lights: 1:28,

M

Making a Difference: 4:28,10:30,
The Main Thing: 2:16,
Maturity: 5:18,
The Measure of a Person: 2:15,
Middle Ground: 7:26,
The Mind: 10:31,
Miracles: 1:29, 3:1, 6:28, 12:17,
Modesty: 11:12,
The Moment: 11:5,
Moods: 5:31,
Morality: 1:23, 3:9, 6:22,
Mosaic- not Melting Pot: 1:10,
Mystery: 1:30, 2:18, 4:30, 6:2, 12:31,

N

Native American: 2:13, 3:21,
Nature: 5:15,
Neutrality: 10:10,
New Eyes: 1:26,

O
Obstacles: 2:22,
Openness: 5:16, 5:29, 6:1, 7:2,
Opinions: 12:20,
Order: 10:30,
Ordinary Moments: 3:14,
Overcoming: 5:4,

P
Passion: 12:27,
The Past: 1:1, 2:20, 12:8,
The Path: 3:23, 8:18, 9:3 (to God), 9:27 (making paths), 12:1,
Patience: 8:10, 8:29,
Peace: 1:17, 1:19, 2:27, 2:31, 3:6, 4:18, 4:26, 7:9, 10:25, 12:6,
People: 12:10,
Perceptions: 10:14,
Persistence: 9:18,
Planning: 4:28, 5:16, 8:7, 8:27,
Planting: 1:22, 9:24, 10:31, 11:7,
Play: 3:3,
The Poor: 10:20,
Power: 3:8, 4:14, 7:28,
Practice: 2:7, 12:30,
Prayer: 4:10, 4:21, 6:13, 9:15, 9:16, 11:18, 11:27,
Present Moment: 1:1, 1:5, 2:5, 5:17, 10:3,
Problems: 11:22,
Promises: 10:29 (broken),

Puzzle Pieces: 5:12, 12:10,

Q
Questions/Questioning: 1:4, 4:13, 8:9, 8:10, 8:12, 8:13, 8:15, 8:20,

R
Racism: 5:19, 6:5, 6:20, 7:14,
Reacting: 9:22, 11:17,
Reflection: 9:1,
Regrets: 11:24,
Religion/ Religious: 4:22, 5:5, 7:15, 7:29, 8:3, 9:6, 9:11, 9:14, 9:17, 9:19, 9:25, 10:11, 11:14, 12:31,
Resentment: 7:5,
Resistance: 7:20,
Respect: 4:25,
Responsibility: 4:12, 5:26,
Rest: 5:20,
The Rich: 10:20,
Risking: 1:13, 2:14,
Rivers: 8:17,

S
Sacred Moments: 1:18, 5:22,
Sacrifice: 2:12, 4:12,
Safety: 6:25, 8:1, 11:4,
Salvation: 9:12,
Saints: 3:25, 10:23,
Sanctuary: 11:4,

Scriptures: 4:25, 12:9
The Sea: 8:2,
Security: 4:9, 4:14, 6:15,
Seeing: 7:7, 7:23, 8:25,
Self-Examination: 6:10, 8:26, 9:4 (self-exploration), 12:6,
Self-Improvement: 9:19,
Separateness: 4:17,
Serving Others: 9:30,
Shake Hands: 5:29,
Sharing: 10:26,
Silence: 7:1, 7:19, 11:31, 12:24,
Simplicity: 8:29, 11:20,
Sin: 2:10, 9:12, 10:23 (sinners),
Singing: 11:8,
Size vs. Might: 7:17,
Snowflakes: 4:26, 5:26,
Society: 8:1,
Solitude: 9:2, 9:11,
Solutions: 11:22,
Sorrow: 10:17,
The Soul: 3:24, 4:31,
Spaceship Earth: 10:8,
The Spiritual Life: 2:29, 7:3, 8:23, 9:3, 9:13,
Stained Glass: 8:31,
Stories: 8:30, 9:17, 12:3, 12:15,
Success: 10:21, 11:11, 12:12,
Suffering: 11:27,
Superiority: 2:11,
The Sun: 5:2,

Surrender: 4:4,
Suspicion: 6:7,

T
Talents: 2:30, 6:3,
Talk: 10:29,
Teaching: 8:2,
Temples: 11:29,
Theology: 6:22,
Thinking: 7:7, 8:6 (change your thinking), 8:24 (free thinkers),
Thoughts: 8:22, 9:27,
Three Gates: 7:11,
Time: 1:31, 3:29, 4:6, 6:4 (how we spend time), 8:13,
Today: 1:24,
Tolerance: 4:27, 5:11, 6:31,
Tomorrow: 1:24,
Transformation: 7:15, 9:25,
Truth: 2:18, 7:11, 7:24, 8:14, 8:15, 9:6, 11:13, 11:19, 12:7,
Tutu, Desmond: 7:14,

U
Understanding: 1:9, 6:23, 7:4, 7:12,
Uniqueness: 10:21,
Unity: 3:11,
The Universe: 3:31, 4:2, 9:4,
Usefulness: 5:13, 9:7,

V
Values: 11:13, 8:22,
Violence: 2:31,
Vision: 5:3, 5:8
The Voice Inside: 1:25, 2:24, 9:1 (still small voice), 11:16, 12:26, 12:28,
Vulnerable: 6:2, 6:8,

W
War: 2:31,
Water: 9:18,
The Weak: 7:22, 11:18 (weakness),
Web of All Existence: 3:15, 4:17, 5:24, 11:3,
Weavings: 4:15,
What We Leave Behind: 10:7,
Wild Forces Within: 11:10,
Wisdom: 1:14, 1:27, 4:14, 5:7, 5:10, 5:23, 11:1, 11:21,12:2,
Wonder: 6:1,
Words: 8:22,
Work: 3:2, 5:20, 9:7, 9:10, 12:29,
Working Together: 4:15,
Worship: 6:13,

Y
Yes: 1:21,

Used with permission from the author:

Go in Peace by Mark Belletini, page 181

The Key to Hospitality by Susan Ely, page 193   (http://thesharedtable.com)

Great Gaia by Ben Stallings, page 182

Go in Peace and Live with Intention by Ben Wallace, page 179

Go in Peace and Compassion by Ben Wallace, page 182

Turning to One Another by Meg Wheatley, page 178

Building the Dream by Maria Wilson, page 184

Used with permission from the publisher:

This Creative Day—When Giving Thanks (on page 236) is from Prayers to an Evolutionary God © 2004 by William Cleary, Afterward by Diarmuid O'Murchu. Permission granted by SkyLight Paths Publishing, www.skylightpaths.com

www.ingramcontent.com/pod-product-compliance
Lightning Source LLC
Chambersburg PA
CBHW071314150426
43191CB00007B/615